all the broken places

*The story of a shattered life,
repaired by God's love*

Rita Newell

FREILING
PUBLISHING

Published by Freiling Publishing, a division of Freiling Agency, LLC.

P.O. Box 1264,
Warrenton, VA 20188

www.FreilingPublishing.com

ISBN 978-1-950948-47-5

Printed in the United States of America

Why is it that some children raised in the most terrible circumstances and who endure unfathomable abusive treatment are able to move on to live satisfying lives? This question remains one that is asked more often than not, and certainly one that I asked myself as a caseworker when I met Rita (Ronni) in the early 70s. First and foremost, I believe that somewhere deep inside, there was a desire not to let circumstances dictate her future. However, I also believe that along the way, there were some very concerned people that believed in her and what might be possible. They obviously felt that caring and acceptance would make a difference in her life. Having been there for Rita through many difficult and trying times while her caseworker, I can attest to the truth of her story of abuse which began as a young child and continued into adolescence.

Barbara Sands

Barbara L. Sands
Former Caseworker November 18, 2016

ACKNOWLEDGEMENTS

It is impossible to tackle this type of endeavor without those who help with various aspects of the research, the editing, and the publishing process.

To my Lord and Savior, Jesus Christ, I thank You for getting through to me and calling me out of a life of darkness and pain and showing me a better way to live and think and believe. It is because of You and all that You have done for me that I have the freedom to tell my story. May it bring glory to Your Name, for without Your divine intervention in my life, I wouldn't be here to tell my story, and it wouldn't have a happy ending.

Thank you to my husband, Bob, for the innumerable sacrifices you have made on my behalf since I have known you. In particular, when I first tackled the writing of the book, you came home to a wife who had been crying all day while I worked on writing my story, and you took everything in stride. Your encouragement through all the years I have been working on this book has been steadfast. I truly couldn't have done it without your moral support and your words of life you spoke to me throughout this painful process.

I thank my former caseworker, Barbara Sands, for her encouragement to tell my story and for her intervention and help when I was a ward of the State of Virginia. I was an angry mess and a handful when she was working with me, yet I knew her support beyond her legal responsibility for me.

I thank counselors and staff from The Runaway House and the Second House in Washington, D.C. for their efforts to help me get my life straightened out. I know I was a challenge on many levels in those days. Thank you for your perseverance.

I thank Robert and Dawn McLain of the Arlington County Emergency Receiving Home for taking me in and helping me as much as you could. You had your own family to care for, and yet you opened your home to some emotionally needy kids.

I thank Daddy and Mama McQuaide for taking me into their home when they were still raising the last of their 11 children. Thank you for making a place for me and for the love you showed me from the start.

I thank Kim Bonham, LCSW, Resource Family Coordinator with Arlington County DHS, for scheduling an appointment for me and making my records available as I researched my own case records to write my story.

I thank Judy Hays for her insights and help as I sought to make peace with my past. I had other counselors who I sought out and met with through the years, and I appreciated your kindness, patience, insight, and prayers.

I thank Linda Barker, my first professional copy editor, who helped me with grammar, punctuation, and content, and gave me encouraging, honest feedback.

I thank my beta readers. My daughter, Katharine Brown, for your willingness to tackle this emotional task on my behalf in the midst of raising your five daughters. I value your input and insight. My daughter, Sarah Shook, who helped me with continuity issues and helped me think about how I should present things so I could reach a larger audience. Elisa Fuhrken, I will forever treasure the comments you wrote in the margins of your copy of the book to help me. Larry Fuhrken, Patricia Fuhrken, and Bob Newell. You all helped me produce a better-finished manuscript, and your encouragement throughout the process has helped keep me focused and determined until the work was completed.

Thank you to several friends who have encouraged me throughout the years. Your words of life came right when I needed to hear them. You know who you are!

Thank you to Tom Freiling and Christen Jeschke of Freiling Publishing for your help and willingness to publish my book. I am grateful for your support, direction, and encouragement throughout the publishing process.

Foreword

As a little girl, I grew up in the same church where Rita came to first meet Jesus. I hadn't known Rita but had long heard about places like Raiford's Farm, and many of the same people who nurtured Rita's spiritual beginnings played a significant role in the beginnings of my life as well. When Rita's manuscript arrived on my desk, I was blown away by the power of her story. Rita has endured unfathomable amounts of trauma and abuse, yet her story is truly a testament to God's healing and transformative power.

Rita's story brought to my mind the Japanese art of Kintsugi. The country of Japan is revered for its production of beautiful porcelain and ceramic items of great treasure. These vessels are created as works of art for various applications and use. If misused, mistreated, or mishandled, these precious vessels become broken, damaged, and are unable to perform the purpose instilled by their creator. Their value seemingly diminished; they are often discarded or written off as useless and worthless. The Japanese art of Kintsugi is the process of taking the shattered pieces of these vessels and repairing them with gold. The artist sees the value of these precious pieces, cherishes them, and fills their cracks with gold's strength and beauty, making them more beautiful as their brokenness is restored.

Rita Newell was flawlessly designed by her Creator. She was meant to fulfill a specific purpose, glorifying God in all that she does. Along the way, she was misused, mistreated, and mishandled, seemingly shattered by the sin of the world. Her Creator knew her value. He lovingly designed her with a beautiful purpose. When all the broken places of her life were filled with the power of the Holy Spirit, her Creator restored her with a strength more exquisite and powerful than gold. Rita's story reflects the beautiful masterpiece God created when He gathered together the fractured pieces of her life, declaring them perfect through Him. Rita is no longer the shattered pieces of her past; she is a beautiful vessel, perfectly reshaped and resculpted in the hands of her Savior.

Christen M. Jeschke
Editorial Director, Freiling Publishing

Table of Contents

Introduction

Writing this account of my life has been one of the most difficult endeavors I have ever undertaken. My former caseworker told me that mine is a compelling story, and she encouraged me to tell it.

My home was a place where I encountered physical, verbal, emotional, and sexual abuse on a regular basis. According to witnesses, physical and verbal abuse began when I was about six months old. I ran away from this violent environment many times, beginning at the age of 10, only to be sent back home by the authorities to endure even more suffering. It was a time when society "didn't interfere with the family."

I have changed the names of my immediate family members, the nickname my family used for me, and the names of extended family members. My wish is in no way to exact revenge or to cause pain to any who still live with the memories and knowledge of my family roots. I seek no justice in a court of law.

I have memories of many events that affected me so deeply I never forgot them. My relatives have told me about the abuses they witnessed when I was very young. For the sake of accuracy and truth, I have specified throughout this book when I was told by a relative about an incident, and it was not something I had remembered on my own.

My mother had three children in three years. My sister Darlene was only fourteen months older than me, and my sister Renee was born just thirteen months after me. Renee died when we were both quite young. Three years later, Cathy gave birth to the son she had always wanted, Edward Jr., or, as we called him, Little Ed. Three more daughters were born in the next few years following Little Ed's arrival. In spite of the size of our family, most of the homes we lived in were small and cramped, which probably did not help the situation at all.

Three of my five siblings witnessed much of what occurred. My two younger siblings have no memory of the abuses I suffered. One of my sisters was only six months old when I ran away for the last time, and she was twenty-seven years old before she knew she had another sister. It is this author's opinion that all who lived in our home were scarred, some much more seriously than others, because of the abuses that went on in our family.

The first part of the book does not reflect just how truly awful my vocabulary was at the time, but it's a fair representation of my language for my first twenty-one years. I was very angry and bitter, and my language reflected my inner turmoil. Since then, it's been cleaned up quite a bit, but when writing my story, I tried to keep it as authentic as possible without being overly offensive.

Additionally, although I have used the word counselor, it does not necessarily mean someone who was a recognized professional within an organization. I saw both professional counselors and those who served in a pastoral sense within their community, so no assumption should be made that "counselor," when used in this narrative, refers to someone in a professional role.

My hope is that readers who are also haunted by painful memories will know that they don't need to remain bound to a past or a people who caused such overwhelming sorrow, devastation, and anger at the core of their being. Victims of abuse can lead happy, productive lives if they have the courage to pursue the road to freedom.

I was often overwhelmed with sorrow and overtaken with weeping when trying to put words to paper that would convey what I had suffered at the hands of my parents. There were days I was emotionally exhausted as I faced the anger, hostility, and violence that had shaped my childhood. I also experienced even more healing when I gave expression to my sorrow through crying; I didn't stifle the painful emotions but gave them utterance.

And so begins my story....

Chapter 1

Living and Dying at Home

Growing up, I lived in a constant state of fear because I had no idea what might trigger my mother's fits of rage. I didn't have to do anything for Cathy, my mother, to descend upon me in fury and anger, slapping me and pulling my hair, screaming and cursing at me. She didn't need a reason, and I was often blamed for something I had not done. I had to endure the beatings and screaming several days a week, if not daily. When I was about five or six, according to one of my aunts, my mother broke my arm during one of her outbursts.

On some days, being quiet and trying to be invisible helped. I would do anything to avoid bringing attention to myself; it was too dangerous. Cathy called me ugly and stupid, repeatedly. Her constant insults about my looks were puzzling to me because I looked exactly like her. Did she think of herself as ugly? This was a question I couldn't voice for fear of possible consequences. I was a "stupid, little bitch," --her words, not mine, and I caused all the problems in our family. I didn't know what a slut was, another name she often called me, but I could tell it was bad because of the cruel way she spit the word out of her mouth.

I remember being really young and trying to figure out what in the world I had done to make Cathy hate me so much. She was always supplying reasons, but none of her fabrications made sense to me. There was no way I could possibly be the cause of all the family's problems; it just was not logical, even to a six-year-old. I was always trying to determine the real reason, but I never could figure it out.

My parents named me Rita Ann and called me Annie. Cathy told me they called me Annie because the name meant stupid and ugly. I heard this over and over; it became something I got used to hearing. Our parents had us call them by their given names instead of the typical names used by children to address their parents. They had us call Cathy's parents, Mama and Daddy, apparently because we all shared a home at a time when we were much younger.

I don't ever remember Cathy or Edward demonstrating love or affection for me. I don't remember ever sitting in my mother's lap. She never read me a book. Not once did she rub my back or sing me a song.

Cathy was very angry a great deal of the time. Here and there, we might have a couple of days where her anger was not dominating the house and our lives, but those days were rare. I never thought of her as approachable. I rarely saw her smile or heard her laugh. I needed to be as far away from her as possible, as often as possible, to be safe.

We moved so much that I often attended at least two different schools during the school year. In second grade, I actually attended the same school for the whole school year, but we still moved once during that year. We were not anywhere long enough for the teachers to realize there were serious problems in my home. Most of the time, we moved in the middle of the night or over the weekend, and we were given no explanation as to why we were moving yet again. Darlene and I would whisper about it at night when we had been sent to bed; we figured maybe we could not afford the rent.

I was as close to Darlene as I could be in a home filled with anger, rage, and uncertainty. When we were younger, we sometimes lived close enough to our schools that she and I could walk to school together. Those are pleasant memories I cherish, as there were few good memories of life with my family.

Throughout the years, we had Siamese cats for pets. My parents were cruel to them. They would put clothespins on their tails and laugh while the squealing kitties tried to get the pins off. They would use an eyedropper to force the kittens to consume alcohol and giggle like children while the intoxicated kittens stumbled around the room. Darlene and I would cry quietly together in the other room, feeling so sorry for the kittens but not able to speak against the behavior. While Cathy was harming them, she was not hurting me. I felt so guilty for thinking like that, but I was trying to survive in a hostile, angry, violent, and confusing home.

We lived in several states along the East Coast, as far north as Rhode Island and as far south as Florida. In Florida, I remember living very close to train tracks and having to get used to all the noise, day and night. But the worst thing I remember about that house was our water. The smell of sulfur permeated the air constantly. Imagine the smell of rotten eggs always lingering in the air. I had a weak stomach, and I felt nauseated whenever anyone ran the water.

In the elementary grades, we attended Catholic schools as well as public schools. The Catholic schools were more advanced in their pursuit of academics than the public schools. If I was transferring from a Catholic school to a public school, I was usually ahead of my classmates. If we were going from a public school to a Catholic school, I was often behind my classmates. As one can imagine, starting at a new school in the middle of the year presented many academic challenges, especially once I reached the sixth grade. There was no continuity. Because of the constant moving, I hardly ever had the same textbook in a given subject for the whole school year. I suffered academically and also socially. All the moving made it difficult to make friends at school. I was often the new kid, starting in the middle of the year when friendships had already been forged, and I always felt like an outsider, never fitting in anywhere.

When we got to go, church was one of the highlights of my childhood (nothing was ever regular and routine in my life except for school attendance and beatings). One reason is that our parents did not go with us. They dropped Darlene, Little Ed, and me off at church and kept the young ones home. Church was safe just because they were not there. Darlene, being the oldest, was expected to make sure Little Ed and I behaved. He and I stood next to each other, and I remember when we recited the prayers, we would use British accents. Darlene must have figured it was harmless and left us to our play.

Cathy continuously lied about me to others. I had made an A in math on my report card, which was a huge accomplishment for me, especially with all the moving, and I was telling Mama about it on one of our visits to my grandparent's home. I knew she would be proud of me. Cathy told Mama I was lying and that I had never made an A in my life and never would, as I was too stupid to make an A. On another occasion, I was talking to Mama about my experience of being confirmed by the Catholic Church. (Cathy sent Darlene to attend, but neither she nor my father came to this important day in my life.) Cathy told her I was lying about that too. "The church would never confirm someone who has a soul as black as hers," she assured my grandmother.

One Monday morning, Sister Mary Catherine Joseph asked me why I had not been in school the previous Friday. I told her (as you never, ever lie to a nun) that my parents had a huge fight, and my mother locked my father out of the house. Additionally, I told her we didn't have enough food to prepare school lunches for that day. This prompted my teacher to call my mother. Cathy told Sister Mary Catherine Joseph that I made the whole thing up and that she shouldn't believe anything I said, as I lied about everything. Sister Mary Catherine Joseph had been kind to me before my mother told her all those lies, but Cathy's lies changed everything. Sister Mary Catherine Joseph was distant and cold after that. Cathy's lies and abuse had now followed me into my classroom. At one point, I had been free from her presence there and enjoyed school because of it. Not anymore.

Often the beatings began because I was accused of doing something I had not done, and I would initially declare my innocence. One of the things that really stuck with me from my time in Catholic school was that you absolutely didn't lie, even to your own detriment. I told the truth as long as I could in the given situation, but when I absolutely couldn't endure any more pain, I acknowledged doing something I hadn't done just to try to bring the beating to an end. Then I was beaten for several more minutes for lying. There was no way of winning. Who knows how long the beating would have lasted had I not taken the blame for something I hadn't done? Cathy always won because I just couldn't take what she was doing to me physically. So, in the end, I was a liar, in addition to being a bitch and a slut and ugly and stupid. Survival was difficult and confusing.

I would be sitting at the table doing my homework or in the living room reading a book, and Cathy would walk past me and throw a cup of hot coffee on me. Then she would say, "Look at the mess you made! Clean it up, you stupid little bitch!" I had done nothing, not said a word, but ended up with a steaming cup of coffee all over me. At least it was over quicker than the beatings.

Another time, when I was accused of plugging up the toilet with excessive toilet paper, I was fed no dinner and locked in the basement for hours. There was no light on, and I was absolutely terrified to move, afraid I would stumble down the stairs into the darkness and probably kill myself on the concrete floor below. When I was finally released hungry and completely disoriented by lack of light for hours, I was sent to bed without dinner. The hunger pangs in my stomach and the terror in my soul kept me awake for hours.

During one of the beatings, I lost control of my bladder and peed all over the floor. Cathy went even crazier than usual and was demanding that I lick the pee off the floor. I refused and was rewarded with a black eye. Cathy told Edward to take me to the hospital to make sure my eye was alright; they scared themselves that time. I was told not to say a word to the doctor or anyone else. My father would do all the talking, and if I so much as uttered one word, they would kill me and end my useless life. At the hospital, I kept my mouth shut and preserved "my useless life."

Cathy would stand me in a corner and provide my siblings with a plastic baseball bat and tell them to beat me because I was very, very bad. Though they participated reluctantly, they did what she said. I couldn't and didn't blame them; they had no idea what she might do to them if they refused.

From a young age, my parents would give me a couple of gifts for my birthday. Before the day was over, I was often accused of something I hadn't done, and this was justification for taking the gifts away. So my birthday was not a day of celebration for me, though I did enjoy the cake and ice cream. It was just another occasion for my parents to wound me. I never got too excited about my presents because I knew I wouldn't get to keep them.

When I was about twelve years old, Cathy began punishing me in yet another way. She would wait until my auburn hair grew below my shoulders, and then she would cut it very, very short. She even cut my bangs very short, which made me look totally ridiculous. The whole time she was cutting my hair, she was telling me how badly I had messed up the family. Cathy was destroying anything "beautiful and becoming" about me. I was filled with such shame and felt so helpless. I would get up out of the chair when she had finished butchering my hair and see my beautiful red hair lying in clumps all over the floor. I tentatively reached up, feeling my hair, and my heart sank as I realized I didn't have much left. Before Monday, I would have to be brave enough to look in the mirror to see the results, so I would know why all the kids would be laughing and giggling when they saw me at school. People in public places would stare at me. This happened to me about three or four times a year. Cathy tried to make me ugly, and she was quite successful.

Another time, when my whole family was visiting Mama's house, Cathy started yelling at me and coming at me, snapping a belt in the air. My grandmother intervened and stepped in front of my mother. Mama had never done that before. All the relatives seemed to disappear when Cathy got angry and violent. "No, no, no," Mama said to Cathy. "I saw the whole thing, and she had nothing to do with it. Your son did it, so if you want to take the belt to anyone, you can take it to him. You will not touch her. This is my house, and you are not going to harm this child for something she didn't do."

Mama saved me from a beating. I was thrilled! And for some reason, unbeknownst to me, Cathy listened to her, and I was not punished for this incident. Little Ed was certainly not punished for the incident, though I would have been.

For the first several years of my life, I did very little talking. I didn't feel valued in my home at all. If I said something, no matter how innocent it was, my words were twisted into something that did not remotely resemble what I had said. It would surely end in abuse of some form. Being quiet was much safer. No one wanted to hear what I had to say; I had been told over and over to shut my mouth as far back as my memory went.

I loved to write. Writing gave me a place to "talk" safely. I also loved to read. That's how I escaped and survived my insane home full of anger, hatred, violence, and fear. When I was fourteen, I wrote a story in a spiral notebook. I worked on it as part of my homework every night, which is the only way I could get away with it. It was called "The Counterfeiters." I took it to school and gave it to my English teacher. A few days later, she told me if I could get it typed up, she would get it published. I went home excited about the possibility of Cathy's approval. I imagined she might even love me because I had done something noteworthy. She took the book from me, and I never saw it again. There was no praise, and there was no expression of love. There was no acknowledgment that I had achieved something most fourteen-year-olds never achieved. She took my "accomplishment" away from me. Looking back on it, I wonder why I had still held out hope that she would ever praise me or express love to me.

Chapter 2

Edward

Dear Reader: I can't tell you how much I struggled and wept over this chapter. How much do I tell you so that you know how I truly suffered at the hands of a depraved and perverted man? How much of my pain and shame do I let you see without shutting you down and "offending" you? How much do I tell you so that you will know I understand your pain and suffering? My intention is not to put pictures in your mind that you can't shake, but I must confess that getting rid of the pictures in my mind that I couldn't shake was part of the reason I wrote the book. It's not pretty; it's not nice. It's not cleaned up. It's sexual abuse. It's ugly and brutal and will destroy the hearts of its victims if left undealt with. With all honesty, you might want to skip this chapter. Know that my father took from me that which did not belong to him and condemned me to a life of shame, self-hatred, and self-destruction until I met my Savior, my only hope, years later. If this tells you enough, skip to the next chapter. I can't determine how this chapter will affect you. If you read this chapter and quit reading because you're offended and upset, then you miss the wonderful ending. If you're offended, with whom are you offended? I hope your offense is with the perpetrator of these acts and not with the unwilling victim for finally being brave enough to tell her story. If your offense causes you to quit reading, you miss finding out how I overcame it all in spite of the deep wounds that ate at my mind, my emotions, my soul, my heart, and my spirit.

My father, Edward, did not seem to hate the sight of me, and he rarely instigated the physical, verbal, and emotional abuse. Yet, he never stopped my mother. He did not intervene. He did not protect me. Edward would walk in the door from work, and Cathy would say, "If you don't beat her, I will kill her." He wouldn't even ask her for an explanation. He would take me into another room, pull his belt out of his pant loops, and strike me at least ten times with his belt to satisfy the demands of my angry mother.

Edward initiated another type of abuse. I have only bits and pieces of images from before I was about five. I have memories from when I was older that have never left me.

In my senior year, when I lived with my maternal grandmother, whom I grew up calling Mama, she told me this story. When I was five or six and my family was visiting her, she heard a loud scream from me. She ran upstairs to see what was happening. Cathy had broken a chair over my head, and I was unconscious, lying across the bed, and Cathy was holding part of the broken chair, standing over me.

"What have you done?" Mama asked from the doorway.

"She told a horrible, sick lie," Cathy responded.

Mama told me she and Daddy thought Cathy had killed me that time, as I was unconscious for several hours. My parents would not agree to a trip to the hospital to make sure I was alright. This must be one of those memories tucked in the deep recesses of my mind, too horrible to bring to remembrance. However, I am sure the "horrible, sick lie" I had told had to do with telling her about something Edward had done to me. So, I learned at a very young age that I could not talk to Cathy about the things he did to me that left me frightened and confused and disgusted.

One of the images that had never left me was when I was in the bathtub and only about three years old. Edward was bathing me, but his touch lingered between my legs, where no father should be touching his daughter. His was not the touch of a loving father, but of a wicked, perverted man. It was inappropriate and frightening.

As frightened as I was of Cathy, I always dreaded it if she left to go anywhere, even for a few hours, because I knew something far more terrible would happen to me. Although I was young and undeveloped, my father still did things to me that frightened me and were sexual in nature.

I have vivid and detailed memories from my early years which have haunted me throughout my life. Most of what I remember is from around age six or seven or older. Edward would send my siblings to the living room and turn on the television and tell them not to disturb us. Most often, he left me in my bedroom to wait for him.

During these times, he fondled me and made me fondle him. I was so repulsed I thought I was going to throw up, but I just squeezed my eyes shut tight and tried not to think about what was happening. I wanted to scream for help. But there was no one to hear me and no one to make him stop. I washed my hands afterward to try and get the smell of him off of me. It seemed they were never clean after that, no matter how often I washed them.

One time he came and actually took me out of school when my mother was visiting one of her aunts. He told the nuns I had a dental appointment. He took me into their bedroom, which was pretty much off-limits to us kids, and he had never done that before. I was very disturbed at being in their room, where I didn't belong. He had me undress completely. That was bad enough, but what he did next was truly the worse memory of my childhood. He forced me to perform oral sex on him while he was performing oral sex on me. I was literally gagging and trying not to throw up throughout the process. He satisfied his perverse appetites with no regard or awareness of how disgusted and repulsed I was by him.

What he forced upon me that morning damaged me deeply. Cathy and Edward had done so many things that caused me incredible pain. There was a deep aching in my heart as the memory of what had happened played over and over in my mind for weeks afterward.

He got dressed and told me to get dressed. Edward told me when the rest of the family came home--I was to say the nuns sent me home from school because I was sick. He went downstairs to play with his electric trains.

I went and took a shower, scrubbing my body wherever he had touched me, trying to get anything of him off of my skin. I brushed my teeth vigorously, trying to erase a memory that wouldn't go away no matter how long I stood at that bathroom sink. I went to my bed, where I cried myself to sleep, blanketed in shame and a heaviness that would impact the direction of my life for years to come. I was trapped and saw no way out.

Before that day, I had been safe as long as I was at school. I could actually emotionally rest while I was at school. I think school is one of the few places I could go where I didn't feel like I was holding my breath, waiting for something bad to happen. I could breathe normally. I didn't have to be on guard at all times. No one at school was hurting me in horrible ways. He took me from my place of safety, and I could never know what to expect after that.

These things usually happened while my mother was out of the house for a few hours or a couple of days when she left to visit her family over the weekend. But one time, he told my mother he needed my help with a cleaning project in the basement. Once in the basement, he set me up on a table, telling me I had to be quiet while he raped me, penetrating me and taking my virginity from me. He was hurting me, but there was nothing I knew to do to make him stop. I just tried to shut down my brain, my thoughts, and all my emotions while he was doing this. I was trying not to feel, but the pain was excruciating.

I thought about screaming while he was inside me so he would be caught, but I was afraid of what he would do to me if I made any noise. And I had no reason to believe I would find any help or support from my mother. The one time I tried to tell her what he was doing to me, he had reminded me repeatedly, she almost killed me, and she would never, ever believe my word against his.

I feared and hated Edward even more after that incident in the basement. He had become totally unpredictable. I was no longer safe from his advances, even when Cathy was home. I began once again to plan to run away from this frightening home for good, never to return.

I started to run away more often, trying to escape the pain that plagued me on a daily basis. Sometimes I would be gone for two or three days before I got caught. While at the police station, I would tell them about some of the verbal, emotional, and physical abuse that I had suffered, yet they still called my parents and had them come pick me up. I was kept in another room while they talked privately to my parents.

I don't know what my parents told them, but it appeared that the police certainly took their word over mine. I couldn't understand why the police didn't help me but instead sent me back to that dangerous home. If the accounts I had shared did not convince them that I shouldn't be returned to my parents, there was no way I could risk telling them that Edward was abusing me sexually as well. I feared they would lock me up and throw away the key, just as Edward had warned me.

Mama got upset knowing I was running away, and she expressed concerns about my safety. "Come here when you have to leave," she would plead with me.

"Mama, this is the first place they will look for me, and I don't want to be found," I replied.

Each time I ran away, we would move within the next few days. We didn't stay anywhere long enough for the police to figure out that something terribly inappropriate and wrong was going on in our home. I don't believe I ever ran away in the same city twice, so the local police were not seeing the pattern with my family. These things took place years before law enforcement offices in different counties and states could communicate via the advanced technology we now have.

We were almost never allowed to stay at the home of someone else unless Edward and Cathy were staying there as well. On one such rare occasion, my parents dropped Darlene and me off to spend the night at Uncle Sean and Aunt Glenna's home. I don't know where everyone else was or why we were allowed to stay there. I lay awake in the bed long after Darlene was sound asleep, and the house was quiet. I felt safe while I was there because Edward and Cathy were not. There was almost a tangible relief. I could breathe normally and didn't have to hold my breath.

"God, I need to know if You are real," I whispered into the dark room. "Things are really bad, and I don't know what is going to happen, but something has to change. If You are real, I need You to show me." Suddenly I was filled from the inside out with a peace I had never known. At that moment, my prayer was answered because His presence enveloped me as I fell asleep with a fresh hope inside me that things could change and be different somehow. But I was very, very discouraged when nothing changed in the days, months, and years ahead. I felt like God had held out hope to me and then had taken it back. He was acting like my parents. He had offered me a gift, but He took it away.

Several months later, I ran away again right at the end of the school day, never boarding the bus for home, and spending the afternoon in the woods. I had no shelter, so I slept on the ground. It got very cold overnight, and all I had on were the brown pants, a sweater over a peach blouse, a winter jacket, and socks and loafers I had worn when I had left for school. The next morning, my legs and feet felt like pins and needles, and I couldn't walk. I crawled to the nearest house and knocked on the door. A kind older couple with white hair and glasses opened the door, helped me into the house, and settled me into a chair in their spacious kitchen. I was shivering uncontrollably as they removed my shoes and socks and rolled up my pant legs. The man filled a basin with lukewarm water and placed it on the floor in front of the chair I was sitting on. The woman used a small plastic yellow cup to scoop water out of the basin and pour it down my legs. She also used a washcloth that she had soaked in the water, gently rubbing my legs with the dripping wet cloth. Her husband asked me what had happened, and I told them I ran away from home and spent the night in the woods. He told me I had gotten frostbite being out in such cold weather overnight. To this day, if my feet get cold, I can't seem to get them warm.

Of course, the couple had to call the police, and the police, knowing nothing about my family, got me "safely" home. Once again, I was severely beaten for leaving home, and we moved the next weekend.

Another time when I ran away, a girl from school said I could sleep behind her house, and she would get me some food and try to help me. She also told some other kids at school about me running away. Three of the boys from my class showed up at my "shelter in the woods" and told me if I didn't have sex with them, they would call the police and tell them where I was hiding. I was in seventh or eighth grade when this happened.

I was in quite a predicament. What was worse, being raped by three boys, or going back home? To this day, I remember their names, Dennis, Ray, and Guy. I closed my eyes and didn't look at them as they took turns having their way with me. I was nauseated the whole time. I wonder if they ever grew up to be mortified and ashamed of what they had done. I was completely humiliated and filled with anger, hate, and sorrow that was so overwhelming; I really thought I was going to drown in my emotions; they were smothering me. I wanted to die. This was the first time in my life that someone, besides my father, demanded sex of me. They did what he did: they took something that was not theirs to take. They used threats and fear to fulfill their perverse desires. They added volumes to the shame that was already weighing me down. I was consumed with overwhelming despair. Why couldn't the ground just open and swallow me, freeing me from this horrible, horrible world?

What is a man? A man is someone who takes from you that which you have not offered. A man makes you do things that make you feel like puking the whole time you are doing them, and then he laughs and talks to others about you as if you were the one who had done something wrong. As long as he gets what he wants, how it affects you is not a consideration or a concern.

From that point on, I learned that I couldn't trust anyone. My "friend" from school shouldn't have been telling anyone what was going on with me; those boys certainly shouldn't have been told that I was staying in the woods behind her house!

Once the police apprehended me and put me back in my home, I only attended that school for a few more days, which was merciful as the boys were telling their stories at school. Their account was not based on the truth, but that knowledge did nothing for me as I endured the leering looks from other boys. Their whispers produced fresh layers of shame upon my soul. Lewd suggestions were made when I walked by many of the boys who had heard the stories. We moved the next weekend, and about a week later I started again at a new school.

Occasionally, Cathy would have a terrible fight with Edward late at night when my siblings and I were all in bed. He had a pretty decent model train set up with tracks, trees, buildings, lights, and people arranged on a ping pong table in the basement. She would smash his trains, and he would smash her dishes. I would huddle in my blankets, shivering with fear, and not wanting to hear the hateful words they hurled at one another. When they thought we were all asleep was the only time I was aware of that Edward actually disagreed with her or dared argue with her about something, but I never knew what they fought about. After they stopped fighting, a weird silence would fall over the house. As far as I know, my siblings slept through the conflict. Maybe the fighting woke me up. I can't really say.

Afterward, Cathy would come and stand by my bed and make sure I was awake. "I'm leaving. Are you staying here with this rotten bastard or coming with me?" she would ask. When she talked softly to me and acted as if we were on the same side, she added volumes to the confusion I lived with on a daily basis. But I wasn't in a position to challenge or question her. I told her what she wanted to hear. As far as I knew, she never asked my siblings that question. Nor did she leave. But my answer was always, "I'm coming with you." If she left, I would be alone with Edward, and that would mean being at his disposal at any time. If she was really leaving, so was I. I had no desire to be alone with Cathy, but the things he did to me wounded me in the deepest part of my being. I couldn't be left alone with him.

No matter how many times they found me, I still tried to run away. I ran away again at age fourteen, but the police found me, and, once again, my parents picked me up at the police station and took me back home. Cathy searched my purse and found a partial pack of cigarettes. She took me into the bathroom and closed the door, lit one of the cigarettes, and grabbed my arm, holding the lit end against my skin until the room filled with the acrid smell of my burning flesh. She wasn't content to burn me once but went up and down my arm with that cigarette burning me multiple times. Then she made me eat the remainder of the cigarettes in the package. I couldn't get them all down and eventually threw up.

A rare highlight of my childhood was being dropped off at Mama's to visit my Aunt Mary (who was only two months older than I) and maybe even spend a few nights. For most of my childhood, we lived three or four hours away from my grandparents, so my whole family would normally spend one night and then come back to get me a few days later.

I hardly knew how to behave in a place where I didn't have to fear Cathy's temper, and I could actually talk and play. On one such visit, I learned about my period. Mary had five older sisters, and she told me the basics of menstruation. Some months later, I was so grateful for that bit of information. If she hadn't told me the little bit she did, I would have thought something was terribly wrong with me when I saw blood in the toilet. Cathy had never told me anything, and when she showed me where the necessary supplies were kept, she didn't add anything to what Aunt Mary had said.

I looked forward to my monthly menstrual cycle, not something most girls would say. I could tell Edward I was on my period, and he wouldn't touch me or bother me. My period made me safe. I wanted to tell him I was on my period all the time, but I was too full of fear of what he would do to me if he found out I had lied.

Once when I had been dropped off at Mama's for a visit with Aunt Mary, I was alone in the room Mary shared with Aunt Susan; they were outside lying on blankets in the sun. I had been there for a couple of days, and the next day my parents were coming to pick me up and take me back home. I was so depressed that I had to leave this house where no one was swearing at me or hitting me or throwing hot coffee on me. I dreaded the idea of going home and the abuse that surely awaited me. I was overwhelmed with the situation and felt trapped. Why couldn't I have a family like Mama's? It wasn't perfect. The girls would sometimes quarrel and yell at one another, and my grandmother lost her temper upon occasion. Yet it was not a home in constant turmoil.

I started crying, silently at first. I was overwhelmed with emotions that had literally been pent up for years; I started weeping and sobbing loudly, consumed by my pain. I couldn't hold it in any longer. The dam burst and I cried for a couple of hours. My sweet Aunt Susan came up and sat beside me on my mattress on the floor with a cool, wet washcloth and wiped my face gently and repeatedly. She didn't say a word. She just brought love and kindness with her and sat with me for a few minutes running her hands through my hair and patting my arm comfortingly.

Remembering the scene forty years later still brings tears to my eyes because back then, I was unfamiliar with the touch of real love. Aunt Susan touched me without inflicting pain, and she touched me without taking anything from me. I was undone. The touch I had known to that point and for many years afterward was violent or violating, never affectionate or loving.

Chapter 3

The Confession

We moved once again after I ran away around the age of thirteen to some small town in Virginia into a single-wide trailer that only had two bedrooms. I was mentally preparing myself for being the new kid at school again and not looking forward to it.

No one had ever told me about the birds and the bees. I had no idea where babies came from, even though my mother had been pregnant several times. Sex education was not taught in our public school classrooms back then and was certainly not addressed in any of the Catholic schools I attended. At my new junior high school, I overheard some girls from my seventh-grade class talking at recess. For the first time in my life, I connected what Edward was doing to me with pregnancy. When I got home that afternoon, I looked for an opportunity to get him alone, a situation I always avoided, so I could talk to him. I found him alone in the hallway at the back of the single-wide trailer we had moved into shortly before starting at our new school. Everyone else was at the other end of the trailer in the living room or kitchen.

I looked him right in the face and said, "I am your daughter; I am not your wife. You can't do those things to me ever again!" I turned away from him and quickly returned to the front end of the trailer, where the rest of the family was gathering for dinner. I hadn't given him an opportunity to respond to me, and I feared he would smother me in my sleep that night. I lived in even more intense fear after confronting him like that. I had never stood up to either of them (other than the time I refused to lick the pee off the floor) and had no way of knowing what would happen as a result. I felt his gaze on me but didn't look at him for the rest of the evening.

I tossed and turned, trying to fall asleep that night. I listened for footsteps in the hallway. I was terrified!

Would my words stop him? I had no way of knowing, but for the first time in my life, I felt somewhat powerful. Maybe, just maybe, he would stop. I would have changed my life for the better because I had taken the risk of challenging him.

I felt safer in the trailer from his advances because there was no basement or anywhere he could take me to do anything when everyone was home. We were literally right on top of each other in that tiny trailer. I hated feeling cramped, and yet it offered me a safety I had not known in a house with a basement or additional floors.

While I was at the Catholic Church one evening for the "folk service," I went into the confessional to confess my sins. I was so burdened by my life and all that was happening to me; I had to tell someone. On numerous occasions, I had told police officers about the abuse except for the sexual abuse, but they had offered no help. I had to tell someone about the ugly secret that was ruining my life. I felt "safe" here because I knew the priest was not supposed to discuss what I told him with anyone else. I told him my father was doing horrible things to me, and I didn't know how to stop it. He asked a few clarifying questions, and I answered him. He was the first person I ever told I was being sexually abused by my father. He was hesitant before he told me to say five "Hail Marys" and three "Our Fathers."

I felt a bit lighter simply having spoken of my ugly secret to another human being, but I had no hope that anything was going to change. The priest didn't offer any course of action I might take besides saying prayers of penance for something that I had not initiated nor welcomed. Someone forced himself upon me over and over, but I was directed to say prayers of penance. I knew enough to not question the priest, and I did as he had instructed me.

A short time after I unburdened my heart in the confessional, we moved out of state and several hours away into another trailer. At the time, I didn't connect our move to my talk with the priest and was caught up in adjusting to yet another school, new teachers, new textbooks, and another new group of peers.

One day as I got up and started preparations to get ready for school, Cathy told me I wouldn't be going to school that day. I was being kept home that day. My father left for work, and my siblings left for school as usual. I was absolutely terrified. This was never a good sign. On these rare occasions, I was always beaten.

"Father Martinez said you have something you need to tell me," Cathy said, sitting across from me expectantly.

I was shocked but figured Father Martinez probably had told her everything, even though he was forbidden from repeating what he heard in the confessional. He didn't know about my mother's hatred for me and her many and varied abuses against me as I had talked only of my father's evil deeds. If he had, surely Father Martinez would never have told Cathy. I told her everything because I figured he had told her everything.

"If you don't believe me, call the nuns at the Catholic school I attended when I was 9 or 10 and ask them if they have a record of when Edward pulled me out of school to take me to the dentist," I said. "You remember that time you came home from visiting Aunt Rosie, and he told you he had to pick me up from school because I was sick?" I abhorred what he had done to me that day, but I was glad for the "proof" that it had happened.

"Why didn't you tell me before?" she asked.

"Edward said you would never believe me," I replied.

"When he gets home from work, I will confront him, and we will get to the bottom of this," Cathy said.

She acted like a loving and concerned mother for those few hours while we waited for his return. Since it seemed like it was safe to talk at the time, I decided to clear up something else that was worrying me.

I said, "Aunt Mary told me that you and Edward had a little baby who died and that you think it is my fault the baby died. Is that true?"

Cathy replied, "Don't be ridiculous. It couldn't have been your fault; you were just a baby yourself when Renee died."

Here was something for which I was not to be blamed. That was amazing since I had been blamed for so many issues that could not have been my responsibility in any way. I was very naïve and began to picture the look on my father's face as Cathy challenged him about what had been going on in our home.

When Edward finally walked through the door, Cathy said, "You are never going to believe what this sick little slut told me today."

All my hopes were crushed with that one remark. It was the same old game, the two of them mocking and belittling me. Why had I trusted her again? Why had I let hope arise? Why had I been foolish enough to think anything was going to change? I hated her so much in that moment! She had held out fresh hope to me only to betray my trust completely.

Her litany of verbal abuse that day was endless, "You are so ugly; no one would want to touch you. It would be believable if he did something like that to Darlene. She's beautiful. You are a wicked, lying, little slut. He wouldn't piss on you if you were on fire."

After that incident, whenever Cathy went to visit her family for a couple of days, she took me with her. She didn't take any of the other children. Edward was never able to touch me again. So, a good thing did come out of Father Martinez calling my mother, though it didn't seem that way at the time.

One night when I was finishing my dinner, Cathy was screaming and yelling and not really making any sense. She picked up one of the steak knives from the table, which hadn't yet been cleared, and stabbed me in the back, and threw the knife down on the table. She didn't even know she had done it. She was sitting across from me, spewing her lies and hatred with her bitter, poisonous tongue. After several minutes, when I could feel the blood running down my back and the sticky wetness on my blouse, I stood up and slowly turned around, so my back was to her and kept my eyes on her face. She went white when she saw the blood soaking through the back of my blouse. She honestly didn't know she had stabbed me. Darlene had seen the whole outburst and had turned white as well. Her eyes got big, but she didn't risk saying anything. Cathy rushed me into the bathroom to clean up the blood seeping through my blouse. She said she was sorry. It was the only time in my life I remember her apologizing to me. She also said I got on her nerves so badly she couldn't help herself, so she still blamed me for what had happened. I wasn't convinced she was actually sorry since she blamed me. Yet, she had also never admitted any remorse for anything she had done to me, so her acknowledgment of wrongdoing left an impression but also caused more confusion.

I knew it wasn't my fault I had been stabbed; I was seething with rage and couldn't express it or say anything, as it would only result in her causing me more physical pain. If the police saw this fresh injury to my back, maybe they would listen to me now. I knew I had to get away from Cathy and Edward. I didn't know where I would go or when, but this incident pushed me to the edge.

"Is she crazy?" I asked myself. Why else would she do these things to me? There was no reason I could think of to explain the constant abuse. I wasn't bad; I was afraid to be bad. Maybe Cathy's insane? She was certainly completely out of control on a regular basis. How could I begin to make sense out of something so far beyond my understanding?

My mind made up; I ran away again, shortly after Cathy stabbed me. This time when I was picked up by the police, I refused to give them my name. This resulted in a brief stay at the local detention home, where I was fed and had a warm place to sleep, and no one was hurting me. I was locked in a room by myself at night. There was a toilet and a sink as well as a bed. I hated being locked in a room, but I hated being home and subjected to my mother's rages even more.

I guess my parents called the police and found out someone fitting my description was at the local detention home because she came to see me and begged me to come home. She said she and Edward had been talking, and they had realized I was more social than Darlene, and, if I came home, I could have friends over and use the phone, as well as go visit friends at their homes. She was behaving nicely to me, and I didn't know why. She was a fine actress when she wanted something. Visiting friends at my home or theirs was a totally foreign concept, as it had never happened, and I didn't believe anything she said. And what friends? We hadn't lived anywhere long enough to make any friends. I ended up going home with her because I had no idea what would happen to me if I didn't. And I hated being locked up during the day and overnight as if I had done something wrong when all I did was try to get away from people who were hurting me.

We moved in the middle of the night shortly after I was released from the detention home in late February of my eighth-grade year. We moved into another house. The living room, kitchen, and dining room were on the first level, which also had a door leading downstairs to a basement with a concrete floor. There were two bedrooms and a bathroom upstairs.

The one thing that was different about this move was that Cathy and Edward didn't send us to school. Instead, we stayed home all day, every day. We weren't allowed to go outside at all.

April was drawing to a close, and we still hadn't been to school or allowed outside. My parents told my siblings that they were protecting me. If we went to school, I would be taken away and put in a reform school. They described reform school as a jail for children and assured my siblings I belonged there because of how wicked I was. But they were trying to keep me safe because they didn't want me to spend the rest of my life behind bars. I had never heard such nonsense! They were doing something to protect me? Not possible. I knew that wasn't the truth, but I had no idea what the truth was.

A few days later, Cathy was completely out of control again. She beat me horribly. Edward was kicking me in the side as I laid curled in a ball on the floor in the fetal position trying to protect myself from his kicks and her blows. Once again, I was the rotten, little bitch destroying the whole family. We were all cooped up inside the house like prisoners because they were trying to keep "my sorry ass out of jail." After Cathy finished beating me, she got the scissors and once again cut off all my beautiful hair. This time she cut it shorter than she ever had. When she had finished cutting my hair, she gathered the two pairs of shoes I had and put them in her bedroom closet. Her bedroom was off-limits to me, so those shoes were as good as locked up as far as she was concerned.

"Let me see you run away now, you stupid little bitch," she screamed at me.

When the two of them were finally finished, they left me in a sobbing heap on their bedroom floor and went downstairs. I could think of nothing I had said or done; it was my mere existence that set them off. She couldn't stand the sight of me, which she repeatedly said during the beating. It was the mantra I had heard all throughout my life.

My siblings were all in the adjoining bedroom and had heard the whole horrendous episode. As I passed the bedroom to go to the bathroom to blow my nose and wash my face off, I saw a couple of them crying quietly on their beds. I felt sorry for them; this could not be easy for them either. No one spoke. The "storm" temporarily subsided, and all of us feared doing anything to ignite my mother's very short fuse.

Why did I fall for her lies and leave the safety of the detention home? She just wanted to get me home so we could leave town quickly. It was only years later that I found out my father was wanted by the FBI for something he had done. If my unusual last name came across the court dockets, someone might recognize the name, and my father would be in danger of being arrested.

Cathy and Edward went out one night shortly after that horrific beating to visit Cathy's brother Sean and his wife Glenna and left Darlene in charge. Cathy and Edward rarely went out, and I felt I had to take advantage of the opportunity because there was no telling how long it would be before they might go out again. While Darlene was upstairs getting the younger siblings ready for bed, I gathered some of my clothing and hid it all in a suitcase in the basement. I was preparing to get out of there. I was able to slip quietly into my parents' bedroom and retrieve a pair of my shoes from their closet; I hid them in the basement too.

Chapter 4

The Runaway House

Darlene and I slept downstairs in the living room. She was on the couch, and I used a rollaway bed that was stored in the closet during the day. I was often awake before the others, and the following morning was no exception. I got dressed quickly and retrieved the suitcase and my shoes from the basement. I opened the back door off of the kitchen and slipped out of the house, quietly closing the door behind me. I was unfamiliar with the neighborhood because we rarely left the house. I picked a direction and started walking as fast as I could. I was fifteen years old when I ran away just before Mother's Day in 1969.

I was consumed with fear. Would they catch me before I got away? Would Cathy sink her long fingernails into the soft flesh of my inner arm and take me back home for yet another beating, spitting her angry words at me as she dragged me down the sidewalk? Would Edward roughly grab my other arm, closing off any avenue of escape? I was filled with the fear of being caught, listening for sounds behind me. I found some woods close to a highway, not that far from the house, and hid in them for several hours. I was determined they would not find me this time. I allowed enough time for my parents to search the area and didn't venture out until I was convinced they would have given up and returned home.

I got out on the highway and did something I had never done before. I stuck my thumb out and stood there until a young couple pulled over and let me climb into the shelter of the backseat of their car. They thought I was a boy because of my very short haircut and my matchstick figure until I started talking. They were nice and were worried about me getting picked up by someone dangerous. Little did they know that I had left "dangerous" a few hours earlier.

At that time, my family and I were living in Northern Virginia, and Washington, D.C., was not that far away. I can't remember the details of how I got there, but I ended up at the Runaway House in Washington, D.C., and stayed there for several months.

One of the Runaway House counselors explained to me that they took kids in with the purpose of finding a solution to their problems and gave them a safe place to sleep while trying to work things out. The goal was to return the kids to their families if it was at all possible or, when necessary, find alternate housing such as a foster home. They did not provide meals for us. We had to figure out how to get food for ourselves. Guys were not allowed on the second floor where the girls' bedrooms were, and girls were not allowed on the third floor where the guys' bedrooms were. If you were caught with any drugs on you or you were apparently under the influence of any drugs or alcohol, you would no longer be able to stay at the house.

The runaways also had to be out of the house every day from three to six in the afternoon. The counselors waited until school was out for the day before requiring us to vacate the premises so we wouldn't have to deal with the police and truancy issues. This was their time where they got their dinner and cleaned up the kitchen and had a brief break from us because they were at our disposal most of the time. Another one of the rules of the Runaway House was that we had to be back at the home no later than midnight during the week and 2:00 AM on the weekends. The house was locked for the night, and if you returned after the established curfew, you couldn't stay there that night.

In an effort to provide counseling services to us, they had a psychiatrist, Dr. Turner, come to the house once a week, and we were required to meet with him in a group setting in the living room. He had something wrong with his eyes, and he couldn't blink. The kids at the home referred to him as "the shrink who couldn't blink." That was something! I thought it was amusing, on the one hand, but also found it disturbing.

I didn't understand why they wouldn't provide meals for us, but they provided a psychiatrist. Food seemed like a more important need.

I told the counselors my name was "Ronni," renaming myself after leaving home this time. They insisted I try to reach my parents by telephone. I was not happy about this and told them I was not going back home, no matter what. They said I needed to at least let my parents know I was safe. I reluctantly dialed the phone number. The phone just rang and rang, which made no sense, as someone was always home. The counselors asked for the phone number, and I provided it for them so they could try it at random times as well. They never got an answer either.

For the first time in my life, living in this place, I ran into a bunch of kids who had stories to tell that sounded like my story. There were stories of physical, sexual, and emotional abuse. Being in that place, I had hope for the first time that someone might listen to me and believe what had been done to me because there were so many who stayed there who had also come from very messed up families.

Because they didn't feed us at the house, I would walk around a grocery store and tear open a package of lunch meat and eat a few slices. Then I would tear open a box of crackers and open a sleeve and put some crackers in my pocket. I also panhandled in Dupont Circle, holding my hand out and begging for money. "Spare change?" I would say over and over as someone new walked by. Once I got enough money, I would buy myself a sandwich from a shop nearby.

Some of the girls staying at the Runaway House had turned to prostitution. I have to say I didn't completely understand how these girls could let men do whatever they wanted to them to get money. I had already had everything taken from me by my father: safety, innocence, purity, and a host of other things. I had been forced to do things that had totally disgusted and repulsed me. I couldn't see exposing myself any further to the perverse appetites of men. I had run away to escape such things. Some of the girls said they were taking their revenge on men. It seemed a dangerous way to get revenge to me. There was no telling what kind of clients one would have, so one had to constantly face the unknown, not to mention sexually transmitted diseases! I also witnessed a pimp beating the hell out of one of his girls when he thought she was holding back some of the money she had earned for him. She submitted to being used by men to get money to give to another man who beat her? It made no sense to me. I had been beaten as far back as I remembered, and I had run from that too. Why would I choose it again? If I hadn't seen some of the consequences of that lifestyle, I might have considered it myself when hunger pangs ripped through my belly.

One day a woman in Dupont Circle asked me if I would babysit for her, so I babysat for this stranger's child for a couple of hours and earned some money. It amazed me that she trusted her small child with a stranger, but I think she could tell I was safe. I loved kids, and it was fun. I used the money to buy food.

Another time I ran into one of my cousins on the streets of Washington, and he introduced me to pot and hash. I had very little money, so I was not getting any of that unless someone was sharing freely. Aunt Rosie's boy and I got high together a couple of times before he got caught and sent back home. The police had been actively looking for him. I guess he told his mother who he had run into on the streets of Washington, D.C. because the next thing I knew, Cathy was calling the Runaway House and giving the counselors all kinds of grief. Yet she didn't send the police to retrieve me. (I didn't understand until years later why she didn't call the police as I didn't know my father was wanted by the authorities). She thought that just by spewing her venom at the counselor, he would be as terrified as I had been and then heed her every word. After a few minutes of this, the counselor handed me the phone, and I told her to stop calling.

"I listened to your lies over and over and came home many times, and I got the hell beat out of me every time," I said. "Nothing ever changed. I am never, ever coming home again!" I kept it brief, but I was an emotional mess. I was angry that she found me and afraid they would come to get me. I was crying and confused. Why do they want me to come back? It made no sense to me.

I had heard all her lies before at the detention center. I knew I couldn't trust her or believe anything she said, so I didn't let her say a lot. Finally, I told her I needed to go. She told me to put "that bastard" back on the phone, so I handed the counselor the phone.

I'm not really sure why I didn't just hang up on her. I could hear her giving the guy hell, and I felt sorry for him.

Shortly after my arrival in Washington, I met some people who lived in a commune not far from the house, and I visited there several times. Someone always had some pot or hash and was willing to share. It was there I met a young, handsome guy named Frank who I smoked pot with several times. One thing led to another, and I consented to have sex with him. Frank didn't force himself on me. It was my own decision for the first time. I was, however, glad that the sex didn't last very long because I was bombarded with images of my father and the vile acts he had perpetrated against me, leaving me full of shame. I was trying to shut out the images involving my father while actively participating in sex, so I could survive the sex itself. I don't know how else to describe it. I was nauseated and shaken afterward. It was not physically painful, but sex wreaked havoc on my emotions. Frank seemed oblivious to my condition, and I didn't say anything because I didn't understand at all what was happening to me, so how could I explain it to someone else?

A couple of weeks later, hanging out in Dupont Circle, I ran into two girls I had met at the commune. They told me they were going to a party and invited me along. I didn't know anybody at the party except for the two girls. I smoked quite a bit of pot and hash, and I began to loosen up. There was a guy named Jeff at the party. He laid a baggie on the table that had several red capsules in it. He said they were called reds and that they helped him to totally relax without a bunch of unwanted side effects. This was my first introduction to hard-core drugs, and I had no idea what I was getting myself into. Relaxing sounded great because that was something pretty difficult for me to do. Jeff offered reds to any of us who wanted to try them. I took one.

There was a guy at the party who called himself Little Jesus, and he kept making suggestions to me about how much fun we could have together and getting to know one another better. I refused his advances and told him I had a boyfriend. Frank and I were not in an exclusive relationship, but I didn't think he would mind my little fib to get Little Jesus to leave me alone.

I don't know how long it was before I was under the full influence of that little red pill, but it hit me really hard. I don't know if it just knocked me out, but the next day I couldn't tell you what had gone on the night before. I had no recollection at all.

When I woke up, I was aware of being naked, and I wasn't alone. Lying next to me under the covers was none other than Little Jesus. He was still sleeping as I slipped out from under the blankets and found my clothes and shoes and put them on. I left the house as quietly as I could and just started walking. Heavy depression and despair settled over me. Why would he think it was okay to have sex with me while I was passed out? I felt used, dirty, and ashamed.

I was walking blindly down the street with tears pouring down my face. Was this to be my life? Why were men repeatedly taking something from me that I hadn't offered? Would I ever cease to be a victim?

This had not been a violent rape. I have heard some of those stories, and they were heart-wrenching. Yet, I had explicitly told this man I had no interest in him or a relationship of any kind with him. He took from me what I had not offered to him. I felt so violated, angry, helpless, and alone.

What was wrong with me? Something had to be since this type of thing kept happening. I was clueless as to how to make it all stop. Again, the shroud of shame hung ever heavier over my shoulders, adding to my burden and despair.

I returned to the Runaway House more broken than when I had left. It was early June in 1969. It was actually during the hours we were supposed to be out of the house when I knocked on the door. They took one look at my face and opened the door. After answering a few questions from the counselors, I went upstairs and had lain down on a bed in the girls' room. I curled up in a ball and covered myself completely with blankets and sobbed until I finally cried myself to sleep. I was physically and emotionally exhausted.

The next time the shrink was in the house, one of the counselors tried to get me to talk about what had happened at the party. I couldn't. The pain was too raw; the wound was too fresh. I was afraid if I opened that door, I wouldn't have the power to shut it again. Best to keep that door shut tight. That is how I had survived the horrible abuses in my home; that is how I would survive this latest nightmare.

One of the kids at the house found out about a religious group that was hiring runaways in order to provide a safer option for earning a few dollars legally. A couple of the kids were already taking advantage of the opportunity. I got directions to St. Matthew's Cathedral, which was just a block off of Dupont Circle, and went to see if I could get a job. I was hired to do some very general office work, making copies, collating, stuffing envelopes, and putting labels and stamps on the envelopes. They paid me $1.80 an hour and didn't worry about how I was dressed, which was good, as I had severe limitations regarding my wardrobe at the time. I worked several hours a week, so I would have money for food and cigarettes. When they paid me, they paid in cash. I remember how happy I was that I finally had some money. I could buy some food instead of stealing or begging. I hated begging. The way some people looked at me was so harsh and judgmental. Others saw me with my outstretched hand and walked in the opposite direction. I hated stealing (probably an influence of being raised Catholic), but I also knew that most fifteen-year-olds didn't have to worry about how to obtain food. Survival was tough.

One day I showed up at St. Matthew's a couple of hours before I was supposed to work. I had been toying on and off with the idea of attending a mass ever since I started working there. So I went in on this particular day and sat in one of the pews in about the middle of the church for a mass being held at 10:00 AM. I was reaching out to God for help--the only way I knew how. I figured if you needed something from God, you should go to church, so I went. I was giving God a chance to help me out in this huge mess in which I found myself. The mass was in Latin, so I didn't understand any of it, and it wasn't helpful in the least. I needed words I could understand, words of comfort and hope. None of the priests felt inclined to approach or welcome the stranger in their midst. There were not many people attending mass, and those who did were mostly older. So, I really should have stuck out like a sore thumb. I looked to be only about twelve or thirteen years old instead of my fifteen years. I was hoping someone would perceive that I needed help and approach me and offer it.

That was the last time I entered a church for many years. God couldn't or wouldn't help me either, I reasoned.

Chapter 5

Attempted Mugging & Trip to Boston

One Wednesday, when it was time to leave the house for a few hours, I asked Jim, another kid from the house, if he wanted to hang out. I was less likely to run into trouble with some of the unsavory characters in D.C. if I traveled with someone instead of striking out alone. He said it sounded like fun, and he wanted to go and explore Georgetown.

After wandering in and out of some of the shops, we got ourselves a decent meal at the Southern Dining Room. I had gotten paid by the church earlier that week and was grateful to be able to buy a meal instead of having to panhandle to fill my belly.

Jim's sense of direction was no better than mine, and we got lost returning from Georgetown a couple of hours later. We asked a couple of guys how to get to 18th and Riggs streets. They said they were going that way and would take us with them. At one point, one of the guys was walking in front of me with Jim, and we were nearing the house. I was engaged in conversation with the other guy. All of a sudden, he waved a huge knife in front of my face before pressing it firmly against my neck and roughly grabbing my arm.

"Now listen to me and do what I say, and you won't get hurt," he said. "Just get your ass down the alley, and we'll have ourselves a little talk. Me and my buddy just want to talk."

I had all my pay from the church in my pocket because I couldn't leave it at the house and risk having it stolen. There was no way this guy was taking my money! I wasn't going back to stealing food or panhandling so I could eat! By the age of fifteen, I had been raped and molested more times than I cared to remember, and it wasn't going to happen to me again! If we were "just going to have a little talk," he wouldn't need a big ugly knife, and we didn't have to go into an alley where we couldn't be seen. Thoughts were racing through my head, but my feet weren't moving; they refused to budge. He was trying to drag me. I was totally terrified but tried not to show it.

"Hold it, hold it, hold it!" I said to him as he was trying to drag me. "Listen here, just—just because I'm a little high from the pot I smoked doesn't mean I can't walk by myself. And you are totally in my personal space! Just get your hands off me and get that knife away from me, and I'll walk down the alley with you."

I spoke loudly and slurred my speech and stuttered some, thinking if he thought I was high, I would present no threat to him. I might actually survive this predicament.

"Listen, here, you bitch! Do what I say, or I'll slit your throat right now," he said.

I could feel the blade of the knife pressed against my neck, and his hand had tightened significantly around my arm. He was getting really angry, and angry was dangerous. But I knew I couldn't walk down that alley because that was a trap and a dead-end and even more dangerous.

"Go ahead and stab me! You will be left holding a bloody knife, and there's a body on the ground, and all my problems are over, and yours have just begun! I'm telling you that unless you get your hands off me and get that knife off my neck, I'm not moving," I persisted.

"I'm going to let go of you and take this knife away, but I'm going to kill you if you try anything! Do you hear me, you bitch?" he yelled while squeezing my arm really hard.

"Yes, yes, I hear you," I said, continuing to slur my speech.

He let go of me, and I took a couple of tentative steps and then started running and screaming and flailing my arms around. The Runaway House was just across the street. I heard him swearing, but I never turned around to see where he was. I just kept running and screaming, trying to draw the attention of anyone who might be around. I heard car horns and saw a car swerving in my peripheral vision as I ran out into the street, but I kept running. Miraculously, no one hit me. Then I was pounding on the door of the house (they kept it locked), and pee was running down my legs and soaking my jeans. I was absolutely terrified. My body had started trembling uncontrollably. Someone opened the door and pulled me inside. I was crying hysterically by now. I had really thought I was going to die! A couple of minutes later, Jim pounded on the door, and he was also pulled inside. I was still too hysterical to tell the counselors anything. Jim had to tell them what happened.

"I don't know what you said, but they just took off running back towards Dupont Circle," he said. "That was really close. The knife that guy had was huge! I don't know what they planned on doing, but it wasn't going to have a happy ending for us!"

The counselors called the police, who cruised through the neighborhood several times over the next couple of hours. We weren't expecting them to find the creeps, but we were grateful to be off the streets and no longer in harm's way. After we rehashed the story to our counselors, they told us that we should never even hint at where we were staying because people would take advantage of us. They also told us the address should not be shared, even to say the corner of 18th and Riggs, because anyone from the area would be able to figure out that meant we were staying at the Runaway House, as had just been demonstrated.

Several days later, near the end of June 1969, I was walking down the street when a young man thrust a newspaper at me, saying, "Quicksilver Times." I had never heard of Quicksilver Times, but I took a newspaper to read later when I was back at the house. I not only read the paper but decided to become a distributor after seeing an ad in the paper. If I worked as a volunteer for the paper, they would give me four hundred copies for free to sell for twenty-five cents each; I could earn one hundred dollars if I sold them all. It was antiwar and anti-government; I had no trouble selling my four hundred papers.

I connected with fellow distributors, Mike and Larry, and ended up taking a trip with them to Boston. I was actually supposed to meet a couple there that I had come to know about through an ad in the newspaper offering room and board in exchange for watching their child during summer break from school on weekdays. I would be out of Washington, and my family wouldn't know where I was, which sounded safer to me. We flew from Washington to New York then hitchhiked from New York to Massachusetts. Mike and Larry were a few years older than me, and they never tried or even suggested anything sexual. They were the first of a few "safe" men I would meet in my life.

We hitched a ride with one guy who took us quite a distance. When we first climbed into his car, I was up front with him while Mike and Larry rode in the backseat. Well, as the trip progressed, the driver began getting fresh and making lewd comments and suggestions. At our first stop to use the bathroom and get some snacks, Mike pulled me aside.

"Is this guy making you uncomfortable?" he asked.

"Yeah, the pervert is pissing me off," I replied.

"Get your snacks and use the restroom," Mike said, "but when you get back in the car, sit in the back with me, and Larry will sit up front with him. Hopefully, he'll get the message. If not, at the next stop, we'll find another ride to Boston."

I had read enough in the underground newspaper to fill me with questions about a lot of things, so Mike and I talked about those things all the way to Boston. It was great not to have to deal with the driver.

When we finally arrived in Boston, we all gave Mr. Pervert Driver some money toward gas, thanked him, and said our good-byes. Mike and Larry took me with them to stay at Russell's house, someone they both knew from college, for two or three days until I was able to meet the connection from the newspaper. Mike really was the first nice guy I met. He wasn't expecting me to have sex with him because he had done something nice for me by running interference with the driver. It was refreshing.

Later that night, I was trying to get some sleep on the couch in the living room. Russell's bedroom was right off the living room, and his girlfriend was spending the night. The springs on the bed protested, and they both were moaning and making noises that left little to the imagination. Mike found me with my head buried under my pillow, trying to drown out the noises. He invited me to his room.

"I can tell you about Boston since we'll be here for a few days, and you really shouldn't have to listen to that," he said, pointing towards the bedroom.

I went with Mike, and he told me some history of Boston. After a while, he went to the kitchen to "get a glass of water," his way of going to see if things had settled down in the bedroom. He came back and told me all was quiet, and I should be able to get some sleep. Who would have believed you could meet a guy like that at an underground newspaper? I never had a big brother but imagined if I had one, he would be just like Mike.

The guys ordered and paid for a pizza the night before I was to leave for the airport. I had heard when you take a road trip with people--it's either an incredible nightmare or a decent journey. I had just had my first decent journey, thanks to Mike and Larry.

The next day, their friend Russell drove me to Logan Airport, saying he had business in the area. The people I was to connect with had told me to meet them by the rental car counters. I waited. Eventually, it was well over an hour past the time I was to meet these folks, so it was pretty evident they weren't coming. I had tried calling the telephone number from the paper to see if I could discover the problem, but the phone just kept ringing and ringing. It seemed to me I had hit a dead-end, and it was time to figure out what to do next. I was mulling over my options when I was approached by a woman, nicely dressed and probably in her late twenties or early thirties.

"Pardon me," she began. "I couldn't help noticing that maybe you're stuck here. My fiancé, Ken, and I are leaving here to go stop by our hotel once he gets us a rental car for our trip home. We're going to find a nearby restaurant to get something to eat. Would you like to use my hotel room to freshen up and then let us treat you to dinner? Maybe you could tell us what's going on so we can see if we could be of help. If you don't want to be bothered, that's fine, but I just thought we might be able to help you out. Does that sound good? Here he comes now," she said looking past me.

I was surprised by her offer but hadn't come up with a plan B, and Ken was approaching us, so I accepted her offer. Neither of them looked like ax murderers to me, and I was usually good at reading people, a skill I developed while trying to survive.

"Thank you. Yes, I would like that. My name is Ronni," I said, holding out my hand.

"My name is Linda, and this is Ken," she said, shaking my hand. I shook his hand as she explained to him that I was going to use her hotel room to freshen up before joining them for dinner.

"Great," Ken said. I marveled that she made plans, and he accepted it with no questions. I had not seen that demonstrated in any relationship. "May I carry that for you?" he asked, pointing at my suitcase.

Wow! A real gentleman, I thought, relinquishing my suitcase. It contained my clothes and toiletries. I was wearing my watch and my birthstone ring (birthday gifts Cathy had actually allowed me to keep), the only jewelry I owned. I was pretty sure they weren't at the airport waiting to steal my suitcase. We drove from the airport to their hotel, and they took me up to Linda's hotel room so I could drop off my suitcase and freshen up. Linda left me with a room key and told me they would meet me in the lobby when I was ready and not to rush. I looked around at all the "personal" stuff in the room a complete stranger had trusted me with and continued to wonder who they were and what they did as I headed for the bathroom to get a washcloth to freshen up. After I was finished, I met them in the lobby. They asked if I would mind eating in the hotel restaurant. I was being treated. It would be great! We ordered our dinner (I was encouraged to get whatever I wanted), and then Linda asked me if I wanted to tell them what was going on with me. She said she sensed I was in some kind of trouble. I kept it vague but told them I had come from Washington, D.C., with friends who were visiting in the area and was supposed to meet some people who would give me part-time work and a place to stay for the summer. I told them I didn't know the people with whom I had made the arrangements, and when they didn't show up at the appointed time, I was pretty sure something had changed for them, and they no longer needed me. I told Linda and Ken I had been unable to reach them by telephone.

"What are your plans now?" Linda asked.

"I have a place I can stay in Washington while I work out what's next," I said. "But I don't really have a way to get there."

"Well, we'll be heading back to McLean, Virginia, tomorrow," Linda said. "Washington is not that far. We should be able to drop you off without any problem, right, Ken?" she asked.

"Sure," Ken said. "We're planning on leaving right around 8:00 AM since it's a long drive. Would you like us to take you back?"

"That would be great," I replied, relieved that I at least knew my next step.

"Ken and I are the old-fashioned type," Linda continued. "He has a separate room here at the hotel, so you're welcome to sleep in the extra bed in my room. "

I accepted their generous offer. Over the remainder of dinner, I steered the conversation toward their wedding plans, not sure how much I wanted to tell these strangers about myself. The next day we headed out around 8:00 AM as planned after they checked out of the hotel. We stopped at a diner for breakfast, and they treated me again. Once back in the car, Linda spent some time telling me a little about them and their lives in McLean and their families.

"I have a younger sister," said Linda. "When she was about fifteen, she had a serious argument with our parents about a boy. That night when we were all sleeping, she ran away. I can't tell you how worried we were for her safety. After a couple of days, she returned home, unharmed. We were so thankful. So many bad things could have happened. We had been terrified. You remind me of her, and Ken is familiar with the story. I couldn't help but think you're in some type of trouble to be so young out here on your own, with what appears to be very limited resources. I thought if I could help you and keep you out of harm's way, it would be my way of thanking God for keeping Barbara safe so many years ago."

I acknowledged that I was a runaway and staying at the Runaway House in Washington. I hoped, with the help of counselors there, I would eventually move into a foster home. I didn't really talk to Linda and Ken about my family history; I said only that I would never willingly return home and that I had been abused for years.

Linda and Ken dropped me off at the Runaway House, and I thanked them profusely for the safe passage back to Washington. I never saw them again. But I have never forgotten their kindness and generosity to a stranger at a time when I really needed some help. I hadn't seen a lot of kindness in my life thus far, so it really left an impression! I was beginning to believe there were some good people in the world in spite of all that I had endured.

Chapter 6

St. Elizabeth's Hospital

I went to visit "Handsome Frank" shortly after my return from Boston, and he introduced me to speed (amphetamines). I had thus far only smoked pot and hash and tried reds (barbiturates) once, which had ended horribly. He assured me that the high of speed was the exact opposite of the red I had taken. He explained that reds were downers and speed was an upper, a good high! He gave me what he called a Black Beauty. At that time in my life, I had a very high metabolism. I slept very little over the next two days because of the effects of that one pill. We smoked a lot of pot during my visit with Frank. I stayed overnight at the commune for two nights without returning to the Runaway House.

On the morning of the third day, Frank announced he was going to be out of town for a few days. He suggested I might want to return to the Runaway House in his absence to keep things from becoming awkward with his roommates. They didn't mind me staying over when he was home, but he was pretty sure they would be upset if I stayed when he wasn't home.

I passed through Dupont Circle on my way back to the Runaway House. Having gone with so little sleep and little to eat, I simply passed out (according to the accounts I was given afterward). My body and my mind couldn't take anymore. I woke up in the emergency room of the hospital, and my stomach was being pumped. The doctors suspected I had overdosed on drugs after talking with the counselors from the house. When I was able to communicate with the doctors, I told them I had taken only one pill and also acknowledged smoking some pot. I told them I thought it was called a Black Beauty, and this was the first time I had ever taken it and had no idea that it would have such an impact on me.

I couldn't go back to the house, as I had clearly violated the "no drugs" rule. It was recommended that I be transported to St. Elizabeth's Hospital for evaluation because no one could believe one pill had that much effect on me. Too much time had elapsed for them to determine how many pills I had swallowed by pumping my stomach.

My time at St. Elizabeth's was extremely scary. It started with my having to strip off all my clothes and have my body cavities searched by one of the female attendants. The hospital had to make sure I hadn't carried anything dangerous or illegal in with me. This very humiliating experience left me feeling completely violated. The search was followed by a shower in an open stall where I had no privacy at all. One female attendant controlled the shower spray while I shampooed my hair and washed my body, and another looked on to make sure I remained in control.

They locked me in a room by myself for the first three days I was there. I was either crying or sleeping. I was in the very place my father frequently mentioned in his threats. Was he right when he had said they would lock me up and throw away the key because I was crazy and there was no hope for me? I was being held against my wishes. Locked in day and night, I didn't have the liberty to leave. I was so frightened. Was I crazy and insane like he and my mother told me all those times? My fear was overwhelming and palpable; these thoughts had been nourished and fed since I was very young!

Then I was moved to a common room full of beds lining both walls. I was only fifteen and, as far as I knew, the youngest person on that wing. There were no other teenagers. The other patients were adult women. I was terrified. I had no idea what the women had done to end up here, and I didn't want to know. Yet not knowing increased my fear.

After breakfast, we would go into the dayroom and sit around in a circle with the psychiatrist. He would ask questions and talk with us as a group. There were several ladies who had been put in this hospital for approaching the White House with a gun, demanding to take their rightful place. There was a lady who stored pee in soda cans in the bathroom and drank it later.

There were women there who knew I would be getting out and wanted me to communicate with members of their spaceships for them. They really believed creatures in spaceships were coming for them!

I don't remember a whole lot about the daily meetings because I was young and scared and worried that my father had been right about my ending up here. Nothing really stood out, except the "doctor" seemed like he had a kind heart. I didn't fear him.

"Sock it to me" was a popular expression back in those days. One day in the dayroom, I was wearing a tee-shirt that said "sock it to me" about nine times. This tall, intimidating woman approached me and was staring at my shirt. Then she punched me in the arm, saying "sock it to me" for every time it was written on my shirt and punching me in the arm each time she repeated the saying. Finally, a nurse arrived and pulled her off of me. It turns out she had attempted to burn down her home while her children were inside.

Most of the people at St. Elizabeth's were taking a strong drug called Thorazine, short for Chlorpromazine (an antipsychotic drug used to treat the symptoms of schizophrenia), which kept them subdued and manageable. I didn't see it improving their situation. They behaved like robots, day in and day out. They had been "shut down" and showed little emotion. I wondered how their lives would ever improve if they were just kept drugged.

I continued to observe the in-house psychiatrist as he interacted with the patients over a period of several weeks. I believed that he was a good, kind, and safe man. So, when the nurse came to me after lunch one day and said it was time for me to meet with him on an individual basis, I was not alarmed and agreed to meet with him. (I call him Dr. Sano for the purposes of my story).

Dr. Sano welcomed me into his office and offered me something to drink. I asked for some unsweet iced tea. The nurse delivered my drink and a cup of coffee for the shrink and left, closing the door behind her.

"Ronni, if I understand correctly, you were at the Runaway House before coming here. Is that right?" he asked. "Would you please tell me how you ended up at the Runaway House? The only way I can make a wise and sound recommendation about your placement once you leave here is to fully understand what has gone on up to this point," he said after I acknowledged that was where I had been previously.

I told Dr. Sano that I had been raped in May after a party. I told him how devastating it had been and that I really just wanted to die because I couldn't handle what had been done to me. I told him I had to "turn me off" to keep my emotions from consuming me.

"The intense and temporarily crippling reaction you had to being raped earlier this summer has me wondering if that was the first time a man had forced himself upon you. This has rocked you at the very core of your being in such a way that I have to ask, what have you not told me? What else has happened to you, Ronni?"

At that point, I told him all about the abuses I had suffered at home. I also told him about being sexually abused and raped by my own father and my classmates. I cried on and off throughout the retelling.

I told him part of me wanted to curl up in a ball and die. Another part of me wanted to punish those who had hurt me. Another part of me wanted to live and make something of my life and show the whole world how wrong my parents had been. I told him that in spite of all my conflicting emotions, I had no intention of committing suicide or deliberately harming myself. I told him I was a wimp and hated pain and wouldn't deliberately inflict myself with pain.

After our session, Dr. Sano concluded that I was a child suffering from a lack of love and from a history of multiple abuses. He said if I lived in a normal home, where I was properly cared for and loved, I would do fine. He told me he would recommend that I never, under any circumstances, be returned to the home of my parents and that social services locate a suitable foster home for me.

He told me I was a strong person to have survived all that I had survived, and he would like it if I would choose life instead of death. He said I should move forward and make something of my life. He told me I should forget about punishing my parents; it would keep me stuck in the past with them when I had spent my life trying to get away from them.

He was a good listener, and the advice he gave me made sense. Dr. Sano gave me hope that I could somehow be free of the effects of my past, though I had no idea how to get free.

I befriended one of the nurses at the hospital and talked her into letting me go outside for a walk. My history of running away had preceded me. She told me she would lose her job if I ran away. I didn't try to escape; Dr. Sano and the Runaway House counselors were working to find me a new place to live. I just wanted out of the oppressive building and to smell fresh air. There were some beautiful grounds to enjoy, and I was surprised they didn't have us outside as part of our therapy.

Eventually, I volunteered to get up early and sweep the dayroom floor and mop it just to have some routine to my day. A lot of the patients rolled their own cigarettes, much easier to afford their habit that way, and they made dreadful messes. I can't tell you how much tobacco I swept up every day, but I wasn't content to sit around watching television all day. There wasn't much for me to do, which made it even harder for me to be confined there.

There was an end of the wing that consisted of a screened-in porch with chairs and small tables. One could sit out there and enjoy a nice breeze and have a sense of fresh air, even though it wasn't actually outside. There was a sidewalk around the landscaped lawn. People who had come to visit patients would walk that way to get back to their cars. I would stand out there and tell those departing that I really didn't belong in here. No one ever listened; as soon as I began talking, they would hurry away. I guess they were afraid of "catching whatever I had" that had gotten me locked up here. I felt isolated and forgotten and wondered if I would ever be moved.

Chapter 7

The Second House

I stayed at St. Elizabeth's longer than intended as my case moved slowly through the courts. Once Dr. Sano affirmed I was in no danger of harming myself or others, the counselors at the Runaway House were trying to get me moved into a foster home in, D.C. Because I had run away from a home in the state of Virginia, a Department of Human Services, located in the city I had run away from, and the powers that be in, D.C., were trying to work out who was actually responsible for me. This made the whole process take longer than it normally would have.

It was finally determined that I would be in the custody of the Department of Human Services of a city in Northern Virginia, and I was assigned to Mrs. Barbara Sands, a caseworker. I believe it was the month of July when my release from St. Elizabeth's was approved, so I was released to the counselors in charge of Second House, the foster home in D.C.

Mrs. Sands visited me there a couple of weeks after I moved in to meet me as well as provide me with her contact information. My first impression of Mrs. Sands was that she was a good, caring person and that she wanted to help me.

The live-in counselors appeared to me to be in their early twenties. The male counselors were Owen, Roy, and Dan, and the female counselors were Linda, Susie, and Debbie. They took turns staying at the house with us, and when it wasn't their turn, they stayed at a house on Q Street. When

I moved in, there were four boys, Grayson, Matthew, Joe, and Derek, and two girls, Mandy and Cathy. Some of the kids were black; some were white. The girls' rooms were on the second floor with one bedroom set apart for the female counselor who stayed overnight, and the boys' rooms were on the third floor with a bedroom set apart for the male counselor who stayed overnight. There were several counselors available during the day, and they had rotating shifts at the Second House.

Mandy, the girl in the room across from mine, tried to kill herself one night about two weeks after I moved in. There was an empty prescription bottle on her nightstand. The counselors had gotten her to throw up working with a hotline agency by telephone and felt confident she was in no immediate danger. They did thoroughly search her room to make sure she had no more pills.

In my new "home," I was introduced to harder drugs such as acid and cocaine. Some of the kids living at the home were from very wealthy homes. Their parents may have had money, but that didn't guarantee they came from a healthy, loving family. I wasn't privy to why they were living in a home, but I thought it had to be something fairly serious for social services to intervene. These kids received a monthly allowance from their parents, and they purchased pot, hash, and LSD, and sometimes cocaine, which they willingly shared with us. My experiences with these types of drugs varied. The first time I took acid, I must have gotten a very mild type. I think it was called purple haze, but I felt pretty good and had some mild hallucinations. Each time I took acid after that, it was pretty scary because I would see things I knew were not really there, and it wasn't tame like the first time. On acid, the world felt very out of control, swirly, and choppy. For example, I was walking outside on the sidewalk, but each time I took a step, the sidewalk seemed to be falling away from me, and I was afraid to put my foot down. It seemed more like an escalator that was going down, and it was moving too fast for me to get "on." I tried acid a few more times, but I wasn't a big fan.

On the rare occasions I was offered cocaine, I said yes. There were no hallucinations, so I didn't feel out of control. I rarely had, if ever, felt peaceful or relaxed, let alone happy in my life, and I welcomed the break from the feelings of pain and anger that never left me. I even let Derek shoot it into my veins with a needle one time, though I hated needles because he said the high was immediate and lasted longer. And he was right!

During my time at Second House, I had to meet once a week with Dr. Turner, the shrink who couldn't blink, whom I had met at the Runaway House. He would sometimes meet with me individually and sometimes in a group setting. Mrs. Sands did advise him of some of my history and the counselors must have told him of their suspicions that I was using hard drugs.

Once, in an individual setting, the shrink asked me point blank if I had used a needle when taking cocaine because it reminded me of a penis. Really? Talk about perverted! Tell me, who was the one who needed counseling here? I lost all regard for him after that. As I said, I hated needles and didn't, in any way, associate them with a man's private parts. When I had to meet with him after that, I always smoked a lot of pot before going. Being high was the only way I could tolerate my private sessions with him. I preferred the group settings because it was easier to hide and forego participation. I was very good at hiding. My respect for authority was already at an all-time low, and here was someone to whom I should be able to open my heart, and he wants to know if a needle reminds me of a penis? Why does everything with men seem to revolve around sex?

The counselors took it upon themselves to help Dr. Turner by helping us to resolve the issues of our lives. Roy and Linda, two of the counselors, came to my room one morning with cases of Coca-Cola bottles and told me they thought it would help me to release anger if I broke the bottles against the wall. One wall was cinder block. After breaking all their bottles for them, I didn't have a sense of release or feel like I had really vented any anger. I felt like I was going through the motions of what I was told to do; my heart was not into the exercise. I thought the exercise was a complete waste of my time, and I personally felt like a guinea pig, which only made me mad. They made me angry instead of helping me get rid of anger.

Roy started pushing me around one day and telling me to hit him. He was in my face saying ridiculous things to get me angry as he pushed me and shoved me. I just started crying, and he surely didn't get the results he expected.

I didn't understand what the counselors were trying to do in these situations, and I went on the defensive. I also didn't know what was expected of me. I do believe they genuinely wanted to help us, but, seriously, where were they coming up with some of these bizarre ideas? Were they learning this stuff in college? Were they consulting with a psychiatrist or psychologist or maybe even Dr. Turner? We were supposed to be living in a home, but at times, it seemed more like a psych ward. The counselors were constantly asking us about how we were feeling and bringing up issues from our past. I didn't know them well enough to trust them. They sometimes stayed in the home, but they were strangers to me. I knew nothing about their lives, but they knew everything about mine. They persisted in trying to analyze me. I felt like I was living under a microscope, and I was being "looked at" all the time.

I had left my home to escape all the horrible things that had happened to me. Yet the counselors wanted me to keep revisiting those events and telling them about everything. It was just too soon; my wounds were still raw.

I saw Dr. Turner weekly. To my way of thinking, that was enough counseling. It would have been easier to talk to him than the counselors because I didn't live with him. Only he made everything about sex, so I didn't really open up to him. I didn't understand why he, the professional counselor, didn't comprehend that I was not emotionally ready to confront my past.

I just needed a safe place to live and three hot meals a day. I didn't want to live in a Psych Ward. I didn't want to spend every day talking about what I had been through. I wanted to move forward, but it seemed like everyone was more interested in my past than my future! It was an overwhelming and confusing time for me.

The Second House was designed with a fire escape on the back that could be accessed from both the second and third floors, and we were probably broken into at least nine times while I lived there. One of these incidents happened when I was in the kitchen making dinner because it was my turn to cook. Linda, one of the counselors, and I were the only two home at the time, and I wasn't sure where she was. I was peeling an onion when I heard several thumps above me. I instantly knew what it was; several people had just entered the house, coming in on one of the fire escapes. I heard at least three sets of feet above me. I quietly reached for the telephone and called the operator asking for the police. I gave them the address for Second House, telling them what I had heard and of the previous break-ins. Then, I ran out of the house as quickly as possible. I didn't try to locate the counselor. That would have put me closer to the strangers who had entered our home, and it seemed unsafe and unwise. A few minutes later, the neighborhood was swarming with squad cars and undercover police. I watched from a safe distance. When they finally arrested our burglars, they were revealed to be only sixteen, thirteen, and twelve years old.

One night I awoke to the cries of one of the foster girls whose room was across the hall from mine. I slipped some pants on and ran to her door, trying to open it. There was a weight against the door, and I couldn't get it open.

"Mandy, it's Ronni. Open the door, so I can help you!" I yelled. I was pounding on her door, hoping to wake up Debbie, the overnight counselor, in the room just down the hall.

When Debbie and I finally gained access to her room, Mandy was naked (that's how she slept) and trembling. In between sobs, she told us what had happened. She had been sound asleep and woke up feeling something on her neck. A tall black man with pantyhose pulled down over his face to distort his features was standing over her and had a huge knife on her neck. She was scared to scream; the knife was right on her neck, and she could feel the pressure of the blade against her flesh. She whispered to him, "Please don't hurt me," and began to inevitably cry for fear of her life. The intruder looked at her naked body up and down a couple more times, then fled out the open window he had used to enter her room. It led to the fire escape. We saw that the window was still open. Debbie and I stayed with her while she got dressed as she was still shaking violently and crying. Cathy stumbled into the doorway, barely awake, and asked us what was going on. The guys were obviously still sleeping since nothing stirred above us. Debbie sent Cathy upstairs to get Owen, the male counselor, on duty that night. Owen called the police, and they came right over. They gathered all of us, even those who had slept through the whole thing, in the living room, and asked us for our version of what had happened.

They asked Mandy if she needed to go to the hospital. She reiterated that he had not done anything to her except threaten her with that knife and scare the hell out of her. They told her she could get something to help her sleep after what she had been through. She declined again. They had ascertained that she had not checked the lock on her bedroom window that night before going to bed. They highly recommended that all of us make sure our windows were shut and secured every night before going to bed. It was summertime, and we didn't have air conditioning in the house. We all had our windows open. That was probably not going to change.

Towards the end of summer, the counselors took us camping in the Shenandoah National Park off of Skyline Drive in Virginia. Once the tents and the campsite were set up, we set off for a hike through the park. It was absolutely beautiful there. We were surrounded by trees, and the wind seemed to whisper to us as it rustled through the branches. We walked under the green canopy created by all the trees, and we continued to explore. The air smelled of pine and earth. For the first time in my life, I felt like I was in a safe place. I could feel myself relaxing.

I remember sitting around a campfire a couple of hours after dinner. Owen was strumming the guitar and singing songs, and the cicadas seemed to be singing with us. The fire crackled and snapped loudly as the flames danced before us, and the smell given off by the burning wood was earthy and comforting. We all had sticks with two or three marshmallows speared on the ends, which we roasted over the fire before eating them.

The next day I was wading in water that was about waist high. I had never been taught to swim. The water felt fantastic, and the weather was perfect.

I looked over to my left, and Matthew, Joe, and Derek were also in waist-high water a couple hundred yards from me, fishing. Their voices were traveling over the water. I figured they were making so much noise; they were scaring the fish away.

Suddenly the rocks in the water beneath my feet disappeared, and I plunged below the water's surface! My body came back up to the surface, as I screamed for help before being completely submerged again. The water was dark, and I couldn't see anything. I grasped for something to hold onto, but my hands closed around the dark, gloomy nothingness. I came to the surface again, and the guys were looking right at me, laughing. I was the practical jokester in the foster home, and there was no alarm registering on their faces at all. They thought I was playing around, and they had moved no closer to where I was battling for my life. This repeated itself several more times as I was swallowing large amounts of water. I had no basic knowledge of water safety or swimming.

Someone must have realized I wasn't joking as my times underwater grew longer and longer. They must have at last noticed the complete panic on my face when I came up. I couldn't even scream anymore. Susie, one of the counselors, appeared next to me in the water and was trying to get a hold on me to help me out of the water. I was so panicked at that point that I grabbed onto her head and was pushing her under the surface, trying to climb on top of her so I wouldn't go under again. She obviously had been trained for situations like this, and I don't know how she did it because everything happened so fast. She had come up above the water's surface and then gone back under the water and kicked me really hard in the stomach. It forced me to let go of her, and I sank below the surface again. When I surfaced the next time, she grabbed me from behind, locking her arm around my neck so she could keep my head above the water, and got us safely to land. I just sat there wrapped in a towel, coughing and choking and in a complete state of shock. I had seen my whole life flash before my eyes while I was bobbing above and below the surface, unable to help myself at all. I had surely been minutes from drowning, and Susie had managed to save me. After that experience, I was absolutely terrified of water for years.

In spite of the water incident, I was really glad that the counselors took us away from our busy lives in Washington to let us enjoy nature and the outside world in that beautiful park. We were invited to slow down and just enjoy life. The counselors didn't bring up our problems while we were in the park. To this day, the woods is one of my favorite places to be!

We were a group of mostly seriously damaged kids and a major challenge. The simplest thing could get so complicated because of what someone had been through living in a toxic home.

In September, I had to go to school. This was my first time in a Washington classroom, and I was one of very few white kids attending. It was a little scary at first because I was in the minority, and I had no idea how I would be received.

Until I moved into the foster home, I had experienced little, if any, exposure to black people. I had grown up with parents who called black people bad names and said nothing good about them. I didn't put much stock in what my parents thought or believed because they had a pretty bad history with me personally. I was pretty sure their views were skewed, at best. I thought it was ignorant to ridicule or hate people because their skin was a different color. All people need to feel like they belong somewhere; they need to be loved and to be appreciated no matter what color their skin happens to be. I didn't think I was better than them because my skin was white. I was there only for a couple of days before any fears I had were laid to rest. Several of the girls had already introduced themselves to me and seemed to genuinely want to be my friend. There was no sense of any hostility from any of my classmates.

Once I realized I had nothing to worry about in this new environment, I was able to turn my attention to my schoolwork. I was a skilled reader and comprehending what I was reading was easy for me. I also had a very good memory. This equipped me for academic success in most of the subjects I was studying. However, with all the moving my family had done and not even attending school in the last five months of my past school year, I struggled in math class and lacked any confidence. I turned in all my homework but earned mostly C's or D's in math.

I liked the structure the school year gave to my life. I had to study and complete homework, so school gave me a sense of focus that I hadn't felt over the summer. It seemed like most of the other kids felt the same way as we settled into the rhythm that attending school provided us.

Because of the new demands on our time with attending school and having homework, the counselors seemed less inclined to draw us into discussions concerning the things we had been through. I, personally, was glad to forget about those things for a season.

Chapter 8

The Abortion

A few weeks after starting school, I began to wonder if I was pregnant. I hadn't had a period in a while, and my tiny breasts had become bigger and were often tender. Although I hadn't really gained any weight, these new developments concerned me. I still wasn't in the habit of asking for help and was of the mindset that it was up to me to figure out what was going on. It just didn't occur to me to talk to Mrs. Sands or one of the counselors or even one of the other girls in the home. So I hitchhiked to the free clinic I had heard about while living at the Runaway House. A pregnancy test confirmed my fears.

I had not seen Frank in several months. He had always used a condom, so the baby couldn't be his. The only other person I had sex with was Little Jesus when he forced his unwanted attentions upon me at the party in June about three or four months ago. I was pregnant with that bastard's child! It was unbelievable! I hadn't seen him before the party, and I never ran into him after that. But it had to be his. The thought made me sick to my stomach.

There was a lot of discussion about what should be done. All of my counselors were advising an abortion. But with my exposure to Catholicism, I knew abortion was wrong, so I argued against it. I said I could have the baby and give it up for adoption. My counselors told me no one would want to risk the adoption of a child of mine because I had smoked a lot of pot and done acid several times. The baby could be deformed.

I was very far along with my pregnancy when the arrangements for an abortion were finally made, still very much against my wishes, but no other options had been suggested by anyone. A hospital in Virginia handled the procedure. Medical workers injected saline solution into my uterus, causing my labor to start. They gave me nothing for the pain. The nurses were angry and did nothing to conceal their disapproval, isolating me in a room by myself. I was completely confused and overwhelmed by the physical pain wracking my body. The nurses only came in every once in a while to check on me. I was crying and screaming in pain when a nurse came in and told me to be quiet. She said I was disturbing the others in the ward who wanted to keep their babies. She didn't know about the arguments I had with my counselors and Mrs. Sands trying to preserve this baby's life. I had not chosen; I had been backed into a corner. The alternative I had suggested had been rejected. I was living a nightmare.

After I labored for several hours, the child was born. The nurses told me it was a boy as they handed me a birth certificate to fill out. I would have to give him a name. I never saw him. The nurse coldly asked me if I was having a funeral, donating the remains to science, or burning the baby's body in the hospital incinerator. She lacked compassion and expressed no concern for my physical or mental wellbeing.

I sobbed uncontrollably and demanded that I be left alone without answering their hateful questions. I had Mrs. Sands' phone number and called her, trying to gain enough control over my torrential emotions to explain what was going on. I told her all that I have written here. She told me she was really sorry that I had been put through such things, but she assured me she would make sure I was not bothered again. I don't know who she talked to or what she said, but the nurses at least stopped saying rotten things to me. They attended to my needs from that point with the barest of communications, just asking me basic questions about my current physical comfort or discomfort and bringing me breakfast the next day. They were still not friendly or kind, but they didn't seem quite as hateful.

I wanted to cry and scream and release the pain and torment bearing down on my soul and heart. But I had already been told to be quiet. I felt like I was totally alone. I had no one. I was always alone when I really needed someone. Once again, I was forced to retreat deep inside myself because there was no other place to go to be able to sort through all of what I had just been through. It was how I had survived so far. Shut down. Turn off feelings. Disconnect.

Abortion wasn't legal in 1969. At the hospital, I was surrounded by nurses and doctors whose worlds had been shattered because they had been forced to participate in the ending of a baby's life. I didn't understand a lot of things back then; I was only fifteen. These nurses were women who helped other women bring babies into the world. This procedure went against their training and their beliefs. I can't imagine the nightmares they had themselves for having to participate in an abortion mandated by the courts. Counselors and doctors called it a therapeutic abortion in 1969. (I can assure you, there was nothing therapeutic about it. Ask any of those forced to participate in mine.) Those types of things didn't happen in the sanctity of a hospital, a place that vowed to protect and save lives, not to end the life of someone who depended on them for their very survival, such as a newborn baby. They didn't know that I had begged for a solution other than abortion, but abortion was all I had been offered. This was not my choice any more than it was theirs.

I was released from the hospital the next day, and Mrs. Sands picked me up and took me back to the Second House. She told me she knew I had been through a horrendous ordeal, but, in the long run, someday I would see it was for the best. As she told me these things, I knew something inside of me had changed forever. Something inside of me had died with the death of my son. I wasn't myself at all. I was very, very depressed and unglued. I had retreated into myself back at the hospital and still had not found a way out. I don't remember responding to much of what she said. I was lost. I found myself in a very dark place, completely withdrawn, and overwhelmed by a sense of hopelessness.

Once back at Second House, the depression overtook me as I tried to make sense of what had happened. The hateful things the nurses had said weighed heavily on me.

Everyone around me at the foster home was acting as if everything was normal when nothing was as it should be! We were sitting down to dinner when suddenly the front of my shirt became soaked. I looked down and realized it was milk leaking from my breasts. No one had told me that was going to happen. I put my hands over my breasts, trying to cover the stream of dripping milk, crying as I fled from the table to my bedroom. I got into bed, where I cried myself to sleep. My body naturally produced milk so my baby could be nourished, but he was dead because of what had been done to both of us. He had no need for the warm milk dripping from my breasts. I didn't know anything about how these things worked, and I was embarrassed as I felt an overwhelming sense of loss even back then when I didn't completely understand what I had lost.

My counselors were also apparently at a loss as not one of them came to check on me or give me some type of understanding in the midst of this awful and confusing situation. None of the kids came either; they probably had no idea what to say or do. The sense of aloneness hemmed me in from all sides.

When I woke in the middle of the night, a few hours later, I was drenched in blood from my waist down; my pajama bottoms and sheets and mattress were all soaked with blood. I knew in my heart of hearts that God was punishing me because I knew abortion was wrong, yet I had let those in authority make a decision I knew wasn't right on my behalf. I was sure I was going to die.

Why had I listened to them? Why hadn't I just run away? I should have called my grandmother. Mama, my grandmother, would surely have let me move in and help me figure out a solution that wouldn't have involved the killing of a baby. We would have either kept the baby or placed it up for adoption. There was no way of knowing it would absolutely be born with something wrong with it.

I was taken to the hospital emergency room and given a shot to stop the bleeding. With no newborn demanding milk, I was told that my body would stop production on its own in two to four days. I was given a prescription to take for the next few days that would help with that process and another to ward off infection.

Several weeks after the abortion, I was taken to see a gynecologist who put me on birth control pills. I didn't appreciate the invasive procedures I endured in his office or his humor to lighten the situation. I couldn't believe he was trying to joke around with me and felt his words were inappropriate. It was more abuse to endure. I didn't expect to see him again, so I kept my mouth shut and didn't say the things I wanted to say to him.

Chapter 9

Christmas Break & Raped Again

Over our Christmas break from school, our counselors borrowed a van from someone and loaded all of us up and took us on a road trip to Michigan. Two of the male counselors, Roy and Dan, and two of the female counselors, Debbie and Linda, also came. We stopped at a restaurant in Middleburg, Virginia, to get a bite to eat late in the afternoon. We crowded into the foyer of the restaurant, which had very few customers at the time.

"Table for eleven," Debbie told the man who approached our group.

"We don't have any open tables right now," the man told her.

"Excuse me," Debbie said, "but you have more open tables than occupied tables."

"We don't want any trouble, miss, but we cannot accommodate your party," the man responded.

"What do you mean you cannot accommodate us?" Roy asked incredulously.

"You can see the sign on the door yourself," Mr. Racist replied. "We reserve the right to refuse service to anyone. We are refusing to serve you. If you don't take your lot and get out of here, I'm going to call the police," he concluded.

It was December 1969, and racism was alive and active in that restaurant in Middleburg, Virginia. We were admittedly a motley looking crew. Grayson was really tall, and he had longer hair than any of the girls in our group. Roy's hair was pulled back in a ponytail. Derek and Cathy were African Americans, and the rest of us resembled hippies. We drove on to a larger city and were able to get some dinner without further difficulties. We finished our trip and arrived fairly late at our cabin near Lake Michigan.

The volume of snow we saw in both Ohio and Michigan was amazing. This was nothing like a Washington winter. We might get a couple of inches here and there, but here it was measured in feet. There were snowmobiles we were allowed to use. We had an absolutely wonderful time flying over the clean snow in the quiet stillness of the afternoon the next day.

One of the kids had smuggled a couple of bottles of Southern Comfort into the cabin, which we opened after we knew the counselors had all gone to bed. We all took turns sipping from the bottle until we emptied it, and then we played spin the bottle. We had a really good time. The whiskey had a nice way of heating up the body from the inside out after we had been out in the very cold weather. All of us kids enjoyed our little getaway in Michigan. It was a real vacation, and we were so much more relaxed on the way home than we had been at the start of the trip.

In spite of our trips to Skyline Drive and Michigan, I was very angry. None of the counselors had come up with any effective means of dealing with the anger and rage that boiled just below my surface at all times. Even if they had, I'm not sure I would have listened to them. Based on how they had dealt with me and the others, I had no confidence that they knew what they were doing when they attempted their various "therapies" with us. They provided a professional shrink, but he thought needles and male genitals were similar. How was I supposed to trust him or take him seriously? I got myself into several difficulties because I tried to resolve things that were beyond me without asking for any help. Life so far had not introduced me to people I thought I could depend on and talk to about the things that disturbed me.

One of the things I had done was try to track down a local FBI office so I could see if I could find out anything about my family. If my father was wanted by them, as rumors had indicated, the FBI must know something. I had skipped school and went looking for the FBI office. The address led me to a very rough section of Washington unbeknownst to me. Thinking about the things that could go wrong and avoiding danger was not one of my tendencies. I often plunged into situations, clueless to the dangers until I was literally in over my head. I lived in and responded to the moment. This was one of those instances. Upon entering the building, it should have been obvious that this was not a local office of the FBI. I kept on, determined to find answers.

"Hello, anyone here?" I called out as I went further into the dark and seemingly empty building.

"Hello, hello," I called again.

I was approached by a tall, large man coming from the end of the hall and told him this was the address in the telephone book for the FBI and I was looking for their office. He instructed me to follow him and led me further into the building. He directed me into a small, empty office and followed me in, blocking the exit.

"What is this?" I demanded.

"Time for me and you to have a little fun," he said, unzipping his pants.

"Are you crazy?" I asked, backing away from him. "That's not happening," I said.

"Oh, but it is," he said, pulling a switchblade out of his pants pocket. "Lay down, or I'll cut you!"

So, I ended up being raped at knifepoint. He held the knife inches from my throat while he had his fun. I was overwhelmed by fear. Was this to be my last experience on earth? Being forced to have sex with a man again? Would he kill me when he was done? My body might not be found for a very long time. No one was aware of my whereabouts, and I was in an abandoned building.

I "survived" the incident and couldn't believe I was being allowed to leave the building when he was done. Walking down the sidewalk with tears streaming down my face, I asked the first person I came to where the police station was and followed their directions. Still crying, I entered the building and asked them to just call a counselor to come and pick me up. They called the foster home, and soon Jean was on her way. It would take her a while to get there. The police asked me what had happened and even went and found the guy carrying the knife I had described. They had brought him in for questioning.

But then I was asked all kinds of questions that had nothing to do with the rape. I was so confused. I had participated in consensual sex in the last twenty-four hours, so this somehow made it okay that this stranger had just forced me at knifepoint to let him violate my body and my wishes? How could they not believe me? My clothes were not ripped. He had a knife! Of course, my clothes were not ripped! I had found myself in a horrible situation and cooperated because he had the knife against my throat the whole time and somehow survived. Was there no justice? He had raped me, plain and simple! And he had gotten away with it.

I went to the police when I needed them and, instead of getting the help I sought, I was humiliated and questioned as if I was the perpetrator in the situation. I was so confused and angry and couldn't believe he wasn't being charged with rape.

Jean made her displeasure obvious on the way back to the house. She told me if I had been in school, where they thought I was, this would never have happened. I had brought it on myself. (I couldn't believe she was telling me it was my fault I had been raped, but that is exactly what she said!) If I had talked to someone about what I was trying to do, they could have made some phone calls and tried to find things out for me, and I wouldn't have been hurt.

The police and Jean were blaming me for something that wasn't my fault. Why weren't they helping me and standing up for me? Why did a rapist get a free pass because I had made some stupid choices and bad decisions?

They had no idea what to do with me, in fairness to them. I was angry, out of control, and making really stupid decisions, though they did not seem stupid to me at the time. I often did not listen to the counselors. I was outspoken, loud, and difficult. Worse than that, I was a victim. I had been a victim my whole life. I had tried to find a way out, away from danger, away from trouble, away from fear, away from demanding men and frightening women. Yet, many of my spontaneous thoughts and actions placed me in the center of all those things. I didn't know how to live as anything but a victim.

Additionally, I believed all kinds of things that were not true, which caused all kinds of other problems for me. I thought they were true. Certain things had happened to me in my life that caused me to draw conclusions. My conclusions were logical and "true" as far as I was concerned because my experiences had proven these conclusions to me. For example, men were not trustworthy. Not one of them. They were interested in only one thing. Another of my conclusions was that the police would not help you. They never helped me those many times I had run away from my dangerous home. They put me back in that place of pain and horror. Now, I had just gone to them again, looking for help, and instead of being helped, I was blamed for what had happened to me. My decision to freely participate in sex the night before somehow made it okay for a guy, a stranger, to demand sex of me the next day, and somehow, they concluded that I had asked for it. No, I had not! But the bastards certainly stuck up for one another.

It was a combination of many things that caused Mrs. Sands to look for another home for me to live in. I didn't find out until researching my records for this book, in May 2013, that the counselors demanded my immediate removal because they felt I was completely out of control, and they didn't know what to do with me. I would have to agree with their assessment looking back on all of it now.

Initially, when I was moved out of the Second House, they put me in a place in Warrenton, Virginia. The people they placed me with had a house and a small motel right off the main highway. It had an isolated sense about it, as it wasn't located in a residential area. I was there for only a few days and realized the owners, who had two young girls, were just looking for a babysitter and some free labor to help with the motel chores. I had been used enough in my life, and I was not volunteering or agreeing to the arrangement. If I stayed there, the only time I would be around anyone my own age was when I was in school. I had been getting used to building relationships with my peers; this wasn't something I ever got to do when I had lived at home. This wasn't something I would willingly give up.

I called Mrs. Sands and told her everything I have written here about this new "home," which would have never been a "home" for me but a place of work. I told her there was no way I could stay. I finally looked outside myself for help. Mrs. Sands told me to stay put, and she would see if she could find a more suitable place for me to stay. A few days later, she called to let me know she was able to make other arrangements for me. She would come and get me at the end of the week and move me to a new location.

I'm not sure what she told the couple about my upcoming departure, but I didn't sense any hostility, and things didn't seem awkward in my last few days there. They didn't even discuss it with me.

I was thrilled! I had asked for help and discussed my concerns openly and honestly, and Mrs. Sands had actually listened to me and heard me and helped me!

Chapter 10

The Emergency Receiving Home

Robert and Dawn McLain ran an emergency receiving home in Northern Virginia, located off of a cul de sac and down a steep driveway. They had their own children, a daughter, Debbie, and a son, Robert Jr.

Mr. McLain worked full time at a liquor store; Mrs. McLain was home with the kids at the receiving home. They did the best they could to help so many messed-up kids. They were kind to us and tried to teach us right from wrong.

Most of the foster kids Robert and Dawn took in were in their teens and had some serious problems. The foster kids came from very bad home situations. The McLain family slept in bedrooms on the first floor. Upstairs there was a large bedroom for the foster boys and another large bedroom for the foster girls. The upstairs bedrooms had two sets of bunk beds and one single bed.

While I lived at the home, there was a boy about four or five years old named Sammie who lived there as well. His mother had aborted him using darning needles in a hospital bed, then walked out of the hospital and Sammie's life forever. He survived, miraculously. Mr. and Mrs. McLain were in the process of adopting him permanently. Years after I was gone, Sammie's hearing was checked at Gallaudet in Washington, and they found out he couldn't hear; they put hearing aids on him, and his IQ went up to normal standards. Robert and Dawn loved that little boy as if he were their own son.

Shortly after I was relocated to that home, Mrs. McLain told me a caseworker would be coming by the house that day, after school, to meet with me to talk about some things. Sure enough, shortly after I got home from school that day, the doorbell rang. Mrs. McLain hollered upstairs, calling me down to meet with the caseworker.

I was about sixteen years old, but I could spot a fake a mile away. Talking to Miss Caseworker at the dining room table, I sensed insincerity, and she couldn't mask her negative reaction to me. I interrupted her in her "this is how this is going to work" speech and asked if we could talk on the front porch for a minute. I yelled to Mrs. McLain that I was stepping outside for a minute.

"Listen, Miss Caseworker," I said, "You obviously don't like me." She tried to interrupt me here, but I was having none of it because I knew I was right. I held up my hand for her to stop talking, and I reiterated what I had to say.

"As I was saying, you *obviously* (I stressed this word even more this time) don't like me even though you don't know me. So, here is what I think we need to do. I'll tell your boss you come to see me on a regular basis if that's what they need to hear, but I really don't ever want to see you again. I'm done pretending. There's no need for either of us to waste our time. Goodbye."

I turned on my heel and went back into the house without a backward glance. I have no idea what she did after that. She didn't come back into the house, and I never saw her again.

You may be thinking that I was a real handful--maybe, but I was sick of people becoming involved in my life uninvited and putting demands on me. She obviously didn't like me, and I didn't need to be around someone else who made all kinds of judgments before giving me a chance. I may not have handled that properly, but at least I was starting to stand up for myself. I knew I had to start doing that if I was going to survive. It was the first time I chose not to be a victim.

Mrs. Sands told me at our next meeting that the woman was just probably someone sent by the court. Miss Caseworker was not from the same agency as Mrs. Sands, and Mrs. Sands assured me I was still assigned to her. I trusted her, and I didn't want to start out with someone new. I was already adjusting to a new home and school situation and trying to find my place within a new family setting, so I was glad I didn't have to deal with a new caseworker too.

Among us teenagers placed at the home, there was a lot of sharing of drugs. I don't remember how we got the stuff, as I, for one, rarely ever had any money. Some of the kids were doing some hard-core stuff involving needles; for the most part, I was drinking cheap wine or smoking pot, and I wanted no part of the needles at that point in time. A lot of the teenage girls who came through while I was there slit their wrists and were extremely suicidal. I didn't understand why someone would do something like that to themselves. Enough pain had been inflicted upon me from as far back as I could remember. Slicing flesh open that produced large quantities of blood and possible death held no appeal to me at all, and I never attempted that. And I never took a bunch of pills; I wanted to live. Many of the girls had been sexually abused by brother, father, uncle, grandfather, or male friend of their father or brother. It helped a lot to know I wasn't the only one, but I was forming some very negative opinions of men based on my own experience and the experiences others had endured and told me about.

Mrs. Sands was in contact with Robert and Dawn, and she knew I was having a hard time emotionally and mentally. She took me to see a psychiatrist who gave me a prescription for Valium. The psychiatrist said it would help me stay more in control of my emotions and help me not to have uncontrollable outbursts. I wasn't good at taking anything on a regular basis, but when I was feeling particularly emotional, I would try to remember to take the medicine a couple of times a day as prescribed.

After a few months, I settled into the new routine at my new home and decided to get a job. I started working a few hours for a bakery on the weekends. Mr. or Mrs. McLain or their daughter, Debbie, took me to work and picked me up. When I first started, I was really tempted to sample all the sugary treats sold in the shop. After about a month of working around so much sweet stuff, it was easier to limit my purchases. The job gave me a little bit of money. Every once in a while, I would buy something to bring home to my "family" with me for dessert that night. There was a black girl living in the home who asked us to call her Peaches. She asked me to see if they had sweet potato pie at the bakery. I had never even heard of it, but I had two with me when I was picked up from work that evening. There were other kids in the home who had never eaten sweet potato pie either, but we all liked it. And Peaches was thrilled. It was small things like this that made us kids smile and made us happier; it didn't have to be something big.

I was also taking driver's education in school and actually became a licensed driver during that time. I had no car to drive, but Mrs. Sands said I needed to learn, so I would know how, when I eventually got out on my own.

Now that I finally had a chance to live, I really wanted to live. I was making a lot of dumb choices when it came to drugs and sex, but they didn't seem dumb to me at the time. I had pretty much come to understand that one couldn't have a relationship with a man unless sex was offered. I figured out that if I had sex with a guy, he would often fold me into his arms for a while and hold me. I loved the feeling of being held, and deep inside me, I was longing for a nontoxic touch. I had not met any men who would hold me like that unless they got to have sex first. I slipped out of the house on more than one occasion when my foster parents thought I was in bed for the night. I met up with Mario, who had a motorcycle and good pot. I met him at the top of the long driveway so the motorcycle wouldn't wake anyone up. He took me to a local motel for a couple of hours of smoking pot and having sex. Then, he would return me to the top of the driveway.

Pot didn't seem like a dumb choice to me because it mellowed the anger and rage I was still struggling with. It had a numbing effect, and numb felt good since I had no idea what to do with the incredible surges of anger followed by the waves of depression. I was still having nightmares and would often wake up in terror. When I had the opportunity to smoke pot before I went to bed, I had no nightmares.

I wasn't the only one living and experiencing nightmares. One of the boys who came through the home had a brother who went off to the Vietnam War and returned home physically unharmed only to be shot to death on the steps of his own home by one of his younger brothers. This boy had seen one of his brothers shoot and kill his other brother. I couldn't begin to imagine what nightmares he suffered.

One of the babies the McLain family received had been held under a hot water faucet by a parent because she wouldn't stop crying. Another baby was left in his stroller in the median of a busy four-lane highway in Northern Virginia. A couple of hippies had heard about the home and drove their van down our drive to the house and dropped off a four-year-old boy and his two-year-old brother. "We don't want them anymore," they told Mrs. McLain before they drove off. Talk about abandonment!

Robert and Dawn's daughter, Debbie, had a friend named Barb, who had a boyfriend named Art. Art was a nasty bastard, and Debbie told me he had beaten Barb on more than one occasion. I didn't know why she still went out with him. He came over one time to pick Barb up from visiting, and she wasn't ready to go as quickly as he expected her to be, and he began talking to her in a very nasty tone and was saying some pretty unpleasant things to her.

I approached his car in the driveway.

"What are you going to do, Art?" I asked him. "Are you going to give her a beating because she kept you waiting? You think you're such a tough guy. Any man can beat up a woman. When was the last time you fought with a man? You've probably had your ass kicked by so many men that you don't have the guts to pick a fight with them. You beat up women instead! How impressive! You're disgusting, and I don't know why she has anything to do with you."

He didn't dare touch me because Dawn was in the house. He told me I would be sorry I ran my mouth off at him.

After dinner that night, Debbie relayed the conversation in the driveway to Dawn. Dawn told me I was really in trouble because Art and his guys would get me when I was off the property. She said that I had picked a fight with the wrong guy. She said I might not survive what they did to me. Debbie said she was pretty sure Art and "his boys" were responsible for the gang-raping of a girl who had run her mouth off to Art.

"As far as I know, at least four guys raped her and slapped her around, leaving her for dead outside. Months later, she's still recovering from what was done to her. This is Art's track record," Debbie said. "He's not involved with the rape and beating, but he somehow makes it happen."

Because of this incident with Art, I don't know if Mrs. McLain was trying to make arrangements behind the scenes to have me moved, but I was really scared after what she and Debbie had told me. Fear caused me to make decisions and to make them quickly. Those decisions involved getting as far away from danger as fast as I could. I stayed only for a couple more days; then I ran away from the receiving home. I was almost seventeen, I was scared, and I didn't even think about calling the caseworker to see if she could move me somewhere or what could be done.

Susan was a fifteen-year-old who had recently moved into the foster home. She said she was running away with me. She said I couldn't be out there by myself; I would be safer if she went with me. I didn't really understand why she would leave the place that was providing food and shelter to go with me. I had no idea where I was going or what I was going to do. Yet, "safer" sounded good to me; I thought, isn't there some saying about safety in numbers?

Susan and I had some interesting experiences over the next couple of weeks. We were standing at the edge of a parking lot of a strip mall discussing our options when a car pulled up. I can't remember what the driver asked us once he rolled down the passenger window, but I told him to go away and stay away. He threw something out the window first and told us we should read it before pulling away. He had thrown out some religious tract all about the goodness of God and surrendering your life to this God. Susan and I had not yet, to our knowledge, experienced much of God's goodness in this life, and we were both mocking the words in that tract. Looking back, it's amazing how bitter we already were, and neither of us twenty years old!

Thirty minutes later, we were standing in the same place when that same car returned. He rolled down the passenger window again, and he offered his assistance to us as we apparently faced some type of dilemma. I was coughing a lot and was pretty sure I had bronchitis. I had been treated for it several times already while living in the previous foster homes. The man offered to take us home and have his wife fix us something to eat. We agreed. He stopped on the way at a drugstore and got me a couple of packs of cigarettes and a bottle of cough syrup.

We got to his apartment, and he woke up his pregnant wife and asked her to fix us something to eat. While we ate the food she had quietly prepared for us, he read to us out of the Bible. He offered to drop us somewhere, but we had no idea where we were going, so we declined. He prayed for us before we left. I make mention of this man and his wife because they were kind to strangers who had nothing to offer him in return. Neither Susan nor I had met many people like them thus far in our lives. It was years later before I was truly grateful for what he had done because, at that point of my life, I had seen little of what I would have called the goodness of God and wanted nothing to do with this God I had cried out to and, from my perspective, had received no answers.

Susan and I thanked the man and his wife, left, and began hitchhiking. We were picked up by a lady who told us she had a house with a mother-in-law apartment, which was empty for the time being. She told us we could stay there for a few days while we figured out what we were going to do. We could come and go as we wanted because the entrance was at the back of the house, and we would not be disturbing anyone in the main house. We stayed there for a few days. We had a place to sleep, but we had no food.

The next day we were out hitchhiking and got picked up by a couple of guys. They were smoking a joint and offered to share. We smoked pot with them, while one of them informed us they were headed to Manassas Battlefield to meet some friends and asked us if we wanted to come along. We said sure. We arrived at the battlefield, pulling up next to the only other car in the parking lot. Everyone got out of the cars, and they introduced us to their friends, three other guys. We were walking on the battlefield; a couple of joints were being passed among us as the evening got rapidly darker.

The two guys who had picked us up chose a spot for everyone to sit down. A couple of the guys from the other car pulled flasks from their pockets and passed those around as well. The liquid burned my throat as it went down, but it also made me feel really warm. I think it was probably some type of whiskey. Another joint and the flask were passed among us until the joint was gone, and the flask was empty. The guys got up suddenly and started running around on the battlefield, making all kinds of noise and hollering. One of them had taken a stick and lit both ends on fire. They were dancing and chanting, but I couldn't make out the words. It didn't sound like English to me. Susan and I were sitting there smoking cigarettes and watching, not sure what to make of what was happening. I figured the guys were stoned and drunk, but at the same time, it felt eerie and sinister. I rationalized that it had to be the pot since it was pretty potent, some of the best I had ever smoked.

"I think they are worshipping Satan," Susan whispered. "I'm scared."

"Well, when they're done, we can ask them to take us back to the house," I said, "but we're stuck for now. I have no idea where we are in relation to the house, but we drove for a while, so I don't think we'll make it back there on our own. Let's just hope they'll help us." I tried to assure her, but I was scared too.

After a few minutes of us just watching them as they continued chanting, dancing, and occasionally screaming in a language I didn't understand, I said, "I don't think we have anything to be afraid of."

I was lying because I was terrified. I felt like I had to say something to keep Susan from being overcome by panic. I was older and had gotten her into this mess, so I was feeling a bit responsible. Who were these guys, and what were they planning to do to us, I wondered?

Once they were finished with what seemed like some type of ritual, they all returned to where we were sitting and told us they were going to leave. We followed them back to the parking lot. They talked quietly among themselves, which was really strange after all the noise and racket they had made out on the battlefield. Once we got back to the parking lot, the guys said their farewells, and everyone climbed into their respective cars. The guys who had picked us up asked us what we wanted to do. Trying to cover up my fear, I asked if we could get a ride back to the house, and thankfully they said that would be fine. We gave them the address, and they lit up yet another joint as we headed back to the house.

Once we arrived, Susan stood talking to them in the kitchen. I'm not sure why I did what I did next, but I felt compelled to do something to protect us. I can't explain how the idea popped in my head, but I went to my suitcase and found the cross necklace I had been given in Catholic school as the prize for reading the most books in a contest our class had participated in. I slipped it on, hidden under my shirt. I can't say why I did that either;

everything was so surreal. When I returned to the kitchen, the guys said it was nice meeting us and immediately left. I pulled my cross necklace out from under my shirt and showed it to Susan.

"Wow!" she said. "I think they left because you put that on. I think they really were devil worshippers. Even though they didn't see the cross, they were somehow aware of it. What do you think?"

"As weird as that sounds, I think you're right," I replied.

"I heard they don't like salt either for some reason," Susan said as she unscrewed the top of a saltshaker sitting on the stove. She threw some salt over her shoulder and told me to do the same. I had no idea what that meant or what it was supposed to do, but I followed her example and threw some salt over my shoulder.

We were both scared and feeling very vulnerable. I told her I was sorry and had no idea what I had been thinking to agree to go to a secluded spot like that with five total strangers. If they had chosen to harm us, we wouldn't have had any way to escape or defend ourselves. We kept checking the lock on the door to make sure it had been secured before we finally settled down to get some sleep. Neither of us was sure that they wouldn't come back.

I thanked Susan for coming with me but told her I thought she should go back because she would probably have better results letting her social worker and Mr. and Mrs. McLain help her decide what was next. I had no guarantees in my current circumstances and thus had nothing to offer. After the previous night's fright, it didn't take much to convince her. She called her social worker and arranged a time to be picked up at a convenience store close to the house. I watched from the safety of the store to see that she was picked up. She didn't mention me to the social worker, so I stayed out of sight.

Once Susan had been picked up, I decided not to stay at that house any longer. The guys from the previous evening had dropped us off and knew where we were staying. I just didn't feel safe. I found a pad of paper and a pen, and I wrote the lady a thank-you note for letting us stay there, leaving it on the kitchen counter. Then, I grabbed my suitcase, headed for the highway to hitchhike to someplace safer.

I was eventually picked up by some guy in a Jaguar. I tossed my suitcase in the backseat and climbed into the passenger seat. He introduced himself as Mac. I told him I was Ronni. I figured he was in his twenties, and he was a nice-looking fellow. He asked me where I was going, and I told him I wasn't sure, but I wanted to get out of the immediate area. I told him I had been with a friend, and we had met some people that made us pretty uncomfortable, so I just wanted to distance myself from this town.

Once I explained that I didn't really have a place to go, Mac told me I could stay in his townhouse in Fairfax for a few days if I wanted to while I figured out what I was going to do. He said he shared the place with two other guys. When we got to his townhouse, his roommates were out. He got out a pipe and some pot and offered me some. He put a Wishbone Ash record on the record player. We both got pretty high. He introduced me to his roommates when they arrived home from work and told them I would be staying for a few days. I didn't see much of them, and they didn't bother me. I stayed at his townhouse for the next several days, sleeping with him in his room overnight.

I did get pretty bored during the day when everyone was off at work. This was before most people had access to personal computers, and I had never been one for watching television. It wasn't good for me to get bored because I almost always got myself in trouble. This particular day was no exception. I decided to go down to the strip mall, a ten-minute walk from the house, and look around at the drugstore. I filled my jacket pockets with little trinkets I found throughout the store. I can't remember what I took, but I'm sure none of it was necessary. It wasn't like I was stealing food to eat because I was hungry. I really don't know what possessed me to pocket things I couldn't pay for and didn't need.

When I got ready to leave the store, the manager stopped me and asked me to empty my pockets. I dumped my treasures on the counter and he had me sit in a chair near the pharmacy while he called the police. It hadn't occurred to me that I was there during school hours, and I didn't look old enough to be out of school, so my very presence had aroused the suspicions of store employees.

I was arrested for shoplifting that Thursday afternoon. While I was being transported in the backseat of a squad car to a detention center, I recalled one of the last conversations I had with Mrs. Sands before running away from the receiving home. She had once again encouraged me that I really needed to think things through before I actually did anything because I never considered the possible consequences of my actions. She talked about how smoking pot and drinking put me in dangerous places and that I already had to live through some very painful consequences. Through our time together, she had been working on getting me to realize that the bad things that had have happened to me might have been avoided if I had given more thought to possible outcomes before I had acted.

"You have smoked pot, drunk alcohol even though you are too young, taken other drugs with no idea how they were going to affect you, been suspended from school for things that never had to happen. You're hitchhiking and have no idea what kind of person might pick you up. You are making really dangerous choices," she warned. "You haven't been arrested for anything so far. I just don't know what it's going to take to get you to wake up. A lot of bad things did happen to you at home that you had no control over. It was awful, and I'm sorry you had to go through all that. However, you do have control over the choices you're making now, and you're putting yourself in harm's way because you don't think. You just do things, and then marvel at the predicaments in which you find yourself."

Shortly after the police had dropped me off at a detention center out in the middle of nowhere, one of the staff asked me some questions and documented my statements. She then had me change into clothing provided by the detention center and surrender all my own clothing. She assured me it would be returned when I was released. She explained to me about mealtimes and activities during the day at the detention center before showing me where I would be sleeping. My room had a mattress over a metal frame secured to the wall and a sink and toilet. I would be locked in overnight. Meanwhile, I was free to pursue activities in the day room until I would join the other "residents" for lunch.

The next day I was transported to court by a sheriff's deputy. I had no idea what was going to happen. I was placed in a secured room until my case came before the judge. Once in the courtroom, I breathed a sigh of relief when I saw Mrs. Sands. I wouldn't be able to talk to her until after court but knowing she was there gave me hope.

Mrs. Sands told the judge she had contacted my grandmother, who had agreed to take me. Mrs. Sands asked the judge to release me to my grandmother's care, promising him, while she sent me a look across the room, that I wasn't going to get into any more trouble. I was going to be the model citizen while I finished my senior year at my grandmother's home. Fortunately for me, the judge honored her requests.

I was taken to a room to meet with Mrs. Sands after court. A uniformed deputy stood outside the room throughout our meeting. Mrs. Sands told me if I got into any trouble once I was moved to my grandmother's home, things would be out of her hands. There would be no other place left for me except Reform School. She had fought for me, in spite of the fact that none of the three homes she had placed me in had worked out because of my choices and my behavior. The judge honored her request despite my shenanigans up to this point. She stressed to me that he could easily have sent me right to Reform School because I hadn't demonstrated that I was being helped by my time in foster care. I was humbled that this kind woman had spoken on my behalf and she had once again been able to make arrangements for me. I was relieved that I was going to my grandmother's home, and I wouldn't have to deal with more strangers.

Chapter 11

Grandmother McQuaide's House

As you may recall, I called my grandmother Mama from a young age. She had what her own family referred to as the first family and the second family. The first family was my mother and her four older siblings, two aunts and two uncles, all of whom lived away from home with their own families. The second family consisted of six more children, four aunts, and two uncles, who still lived at home when I moved in with them. So, I had aunts and uncles that were close to my age or younger than me.

Mama and Daddy's bedroom was on the main floor, and due to health issues, Aunt Denise slept in their room so Mama could listen for her throughout the night. Aunt Georgia, the oldest of the children still living at home, occupied the only other bedroom on the main floor.

The only other bedroom in Mama's house was located on the second floor and was shared by Aunt Susan and Aunt Mary. There was no space to put another bed in the room they shared. At the top of the stairs in the attic, Uncle Matt had his bed and dresser in the corner to the right, Uncle Timmy had his bed and dresser in the left corner directly across from Matt's area, and outside Susan and Mary's room, a few feet down the hall facing Uncle Timmy's bed, they made space for a bed for me. There was no door between my sleeping space and Timmy and Matt's, but I used my bed only when sleeping. I slept in a tee shirt and long pants every night, and I changed in the bathroom or in my aunts' bedroom. My Aunts made room for my clothes in their bedroom closet, and I placed my suitcase under my bed where I stored underclothes, long pants, tee-shirts, and socks. I put my extra shoes under my bed too.

The main floor contained the only bathroom in the house and a living room and eat-in kitchen. There were nine of us, and we successfully shared one bathroom. That amazes me, as most of us were girls. As a result, the bathroom was only for taking a shower, using the toilet, or brushing teeth.

When I think about the kitchen, I am amazed that Mama was able to prepare meals for nine in that tiny area. There was a stove with a little bit of counter space to the right. A small sink was across from the stove where the dishes were washed. There was no dishwasher; the girls took turns doing the dishes because the space was so cramped. The refrigerator was kept on the porch located off the kitchen and dining area.

When I moved in with Mama and her family in October of 1972, I stopped going by the name Ronni. Mama had called me Annie my whole life, and I couldn't ask her to call me another name.

Aunts Georgia, Susan, and Mary were into what I called "girly stuff." They knew how to style their hair to make it pretty, something I had never learned, and they all wore makeup. They fussed with their hair and makeup at the vanities in their respective bedrooms, not in the bathroom. I was never encouraged in my femininity by my mother and had never owned any makeup. When I was younger, my hair was actually long enough that it could've been curled or styled; but it didn't stay that way long because my mother would cut it short. Also, my sisters and I didn't have curlers or things like that. Foundation and powder would've been unnecessary expenses in our household. My mother used makeup only on very rare occasions, and she usually wore only some mascara and lipstick.

While living at Mama's, I attended the same high school with my Aunt Mary, and we both were in our senior year. My education had really been messed up by all the moving, lack of encouragement from my parents, and the total lack of attendance the last few months I had lived at home. The goal for my new school was for me to get any credits I was lacking so I could actually graduate. I had to take a U.S. government course, two periods of physical education, and two periods of English (I took English and humanities). I also took drama.

Mary and I approached school from two different mindsets; she was a very serious student and wanted nothing but A's because she was going to go to college. I was just trying to finish high school, so I could be free of the government interfering in my life.

I was attending a school for the first time, where showering was a required part of gym participation. My two required gym classes were scheduled back to back, so I wasn't expected to take a shower after the first class, but I refused to shower after my final gym class. There was no privacy as the shower stalls had no curtains. I refused to be naked in front of my gym teachers or other students. My sexuality was already fragile and damaged, and no one was going to force me to be naked around a bunch of strangers.

As far as I was concerned, being naked was not safe. The idea both repulsed me and paralyzed me with fear and made me want to throw up. In my own way, I was standing up for myself but hadn't explained that to anyone else. In my life, up to this point, I had the sense that I had to figure things out for myself, and it never occurred to me to talk to Mrs. Sands or my guidance counselor and see if I had any options when faced with this situation in gym class.

I got a D in both gym classes because of refusing to shower and for lack of participation in some of the activities. As long as there was no perceived danger, I participated in the classes. But if I sensed danger, I wouldn't participate. For example, on the day we were introduced to the uneven parallel bars, one of the girls lost her grip when changing bars and fell and broke her collarbone. There was no way I was going to get on those bars after seeing Colleen hurt. I certainly wasn't planning on becoming a gymnast and was unwilling to take an unnecessary risk.

In addition to going to school, I got a job working weekends at a local restaurant as a waitress. Mama or one of the girls would drive me to work and pick me up when my shift was over. This gave me some pocket money.

I also went to church on a regular basis with several of my aunts and my uncles. Mama and Daddy didn't go for some reason; maybe they stayed home with Aunt Denise; maybe it was the only time they had the house mostly to themselves. My parents had sent us but didn't attend themselves, so to me, it wasn't that unusual that my grandparents didn't go. We attended a Catholic church, but it didn't really do a lot for me. In the past, I had trusted a priest with my deepest pain, and he had told my mother about it, thinking she was an advocate. He had been wrong. I didn't listen to people I didn't trust, regardless of title or position. The priest might have been saying something good up there, but I just turned him off in my mind and went through the motions as expected. I was afraid to trust again. He was a stranger. I knew nothing about him except his name. I didn't know anything about where he came from, what involvements he may have had, and what he truly believed about life. I didn't feel like I owed him anything just because he was a priest.

And just as Mrs. Sands had said, I did really stupid things that definitely could have got me sent right off to reform school. On the one hand, I was afraid of making waves. On the other hand, I was stubborn about what I would and wouldn't do. The stubbornness had a deep, deep fear at its root that even I didn't completely understand.

One day, I heard that my mother and siblings were coming to Lynchburg to see Mama and the family. I just couldn't deal with it. I didn't talk with anyone about it. Again, I was faced with a problem that I thought I had to solve. Just contemplating seeing my mother filled me with fear and made me feel physically sick. So, I made arrangements to go home with a girl from school on Friday and stayed away until Sunday afternoon when I knew they'd be gone. I didn't even tell Aunt Mary because I knew she would have to answer my grandparents' questions, and then I would've been dragged back to the house and forced to deal with my mother. And that's something I couldn't handle.

Needless to say, everyone was very, very upset when I got back. I tried to explain myself, but Mama said now that I lived in her home Cathy, couldn't do anything to me there. I knew that being in Mama's house wouldn't stop Cathy from doing anything she wanted to do or keep her from saying anything she wanted to say. I don't know why, but I was unable to make them see that. Mrs. Sands and I had to talk on the telephone. I was told if I pulled another stunt like that, I would be sent to reform school.

There were no mandatory counseling sessions while staying at Mama's. Maybe that was a bad thing because I didn't know how to express what was going on inside of me when fear consumed me when faced with difficult situations. Maybe if I had still had access to professional input, I would have found a solution that didn't upset everyone. I was told to talk to my guidance counselor at school. I didn't see it as an option, initially. My guidance counselor was yet another stranger. Why was I expected to trust people because of their title or position? The people in "positions of authority" in my life had been my parents. They had both proved themselves unworthy of anyone's trust. They had both abused their "position of authority" in my life, and I had been hurt on so many different levels.

However, if I was having issues at school and just needed to temporarily remove myself from a difficult situation, the guidance counselor told me I could come to his office at any time and just have some time to settle myself down. He said he may or may not be in the office, but this was an arrangement he had explained to the rest of his staff. I did take him up on that offer several times. When I felt like I was out of control, I would go there and just sit until I calmed down.

Sometimes he was in, and at those times, he always made himself available to talk. But he didn't push me. If I didn't want to talk, he left me alone. If I wanted to talk, he would listen and sometimes offer his perspective on things. Because he didn't push, I did open up to him about some of the things with which I struggled.

One time, for creative writing, I asked to go to the library to do some research, and my request was granted. I went into one of the "study rooms" off the library, closed and locked the door, lowered the blinds on the door, put Vivaldi on the record player, opened the library window, and went out on the roof and smoked a joint. I loved to write after smoking pot; the music of Vivaldi stirred up vivid images in my mind. After I finished the joint, I climbed back into the library, closed the window, pulled up the blinds, and sat and tackled my writing assignment. The words flew freely through my pen as I filled page after page. When I felt like I was finished, I turned off the music and left the library.

Before the school day ended, I was suspended from school for "smelling like pot," even though no pot was found on my person. I had to empty my pockets, and my purse was searched. No pot or paraphernalia was found. However, I was suspended for three days. Terrified, I lied to the guidance counselor and told him my grandmother couldn't be told as she had a bad heart. I said they should mail the letter to my mother, Cathy, and gave them an address of a friend I had made at school while living at the Emergency Receiving Home who now lived in California.

As far as I know, the McQuaide family never knew what had happened, and I feel certain that Mrs. Sands hadn't been notified either. I'm not sure why. I had turned nineteen in November, so maybe that had something to do with it. Maybe with my grandparents being my legal guardians, Mrs. Sands was out of the picture. Whatever the reason, no one was notified about the pot. I was glad because the consequences wouldn't have been good for me.

For the next three days, Mama would drop us off at school, and I would walk towards the building. I would enter through one door with Aunt Mary, and when we separated ways, I would exit through another door. I would go to a friend's house within walking distance of the school and smoke pot all day. I never got caught, and my grandmother never found out, as far as I know. If my Aunt Mary knew, she didn't say anything. I was at least smart enough after that to not smoke pot on school property anymore and certainly not on the library roof. As much as I hated being locked up in those detention centers, I can't believe I risked getting put some place like that on a more permanent basis.

As far as drugs were concerned, I limited myself to smoking pot while living at Mama's. Once, though, I took some Quaaludes (methaqualone) and some acid. I got the drugs from the people I hung out with while on suspension and other kids at school. When I took the acid, I was supposed to be spending the night at someone's house, but all my plans fell through. I got dropped off at Mama's right in the middle of the acid trip. I was hallucinating and disoriented. Fortunately, I made it upstairs to my bed without disturbing anyone as they were already in bed. I laid on my bed, tripping all night, and had to be quiet in the midst of seeing dancing, swirling, shaking, vibrating, colorful things all over the walls and ceiling. It was very, very hard, but I didn't make a sound because I knew, for sure, that would have gotten me kicked out of my grandmother's home. I had been told there was no place else for me to go, and this was my last chance to do the right thing.

After this incident, I realized how close I had come to really screwing things up, and I began to take fewer risks. I needed to finish high school, so I could move on with my life.

In June of 1973, I actually graduated from high school. Shortly after that, I left Mama's home and moved to the Northern Virginia area, staying at a townhouse being rented by Mac, the guy I had met in that area earlier as a runaway, and his two male roommates. Mac and I had stayed in touch by letter, and he had already said it would be fine for me to stay at the townhouse while I looked for a job and a place of my own.

Mac had known me as Ronni. I asked him to please call me Rita moving forward. With my chance at a new life, I thought a new name was fitting. I didn't want to be called Annie because my mother told me it meant ugly and stupid. I didn't want her identifying who I was and who I was becoming.

Initially, I worked for a dry cleaner within walking distance of the townhouse. But I ended up getting pretty sick with severe bronchitis while working there. The back area, where I worked with the Adjust-a-Drape machine, was very, very hot. After work, I would return to the air-conditioned townhouse. My body was having a hard time adjusting to the extreme temperature differences between work and home. My smoking habit didn't help my situation; it probably made me more sensitive. At the time, I was smoking two to three packs of cigarettes a day.

When I was called and told I got a job with another company, I gladly quit the dry-cleaning job. I had been hired by a local drugstore as a drug clerk working in the pharmacy. This store also was within walking distance of home. At the drugstore, I would open boxes and restock the over-the-counter merchandise and accept payment from customers for their prescriptions and other things they brought with them to my register. I was getting good hours working there. I was saving my money as I didn't have a lot of expenses at the townhouse because Mac and his roommates knew I was trying to get on my feet. My time here was preparing for the day I could move out. Some people seem to really struggle at saving money, but at this point in my life, I was pretty good at it. I knew I would have to get a car and pay security deposits and other things to get my own place, so I was motivated to save my money.

Mac and his roommates would have parties, and a lot of people would come to both drink and get high on pot. Occasionally, one of the guests would share some cocaine as well. At several of these parties, some guy attending thought I was available for sex just because I was sharing a townhouse with guys. While living there, I had to learn to stand up for myself, and I did so with a passion. This is how it would happen. Some guy would start a conversation with me. He would talk to me for a few minutes, then try to start something sexual. Sometimes I had to get physical to insist that "no" meant "no." I was feeling good about my developing ability to stand up for myself, but I also got depressed after these incidents. What was it with men that made them think they could take something from a woman who said no to their advances? If I hadn't stood up for myself in that townhouse, I would have been violated more than once.

One day, I woke up in horrible pain, and I called Mrs. Sands to describe the location of the pain and the pain itself. Mrs. Sands told me it sounded like appendicitis. She recommended that I go straight to the emergency room. I called a friend who picked me up and dropped me off at the hospital. After the initial examination, it was determined I was running a high fever, and, based on the location of my pain, I was quickly prepped for surgery. That was the last thing I remembered. When I woke up, I found out I had been admitted to the hospital, and a nurse told me the doctor would explain everything to me when he made his rounds. I called Mrs. Sands and told her my appendix had been removed, that I also had been admitted to the hospital, and would let her know an update once I got a chance to talk to the doctor. The nurse had given me pain medication and checked the drip bag hooked up to a needle in my arm but would not discuss my situation with me.

The doctor finally made his rounds around dinnertime. He checked my chart and my blood pressure, took my temperature, and listened to my heart, and made some more notes before he started talking.

"Well, Rita, it appears your appendix wasn't the cause of the acute pain you were experiencing. However, since we had already made the incision and you really don't need your appendix, we went ahead and removed it. You have an infection called pelvic inflammatory disease, and by the look of things, you have had it for a while. Because this was not diagnosed at the outset, I'm pretty sure that you will never be able to have children. You have a lot of scar tissue in the area. We are giving you an antibiotic intravenously. If that brings down your high fever and it stays down, we should be able to release you in a couple of days. You'll be sent home with another antibiotic prescription that you'll need to take until it's finished to make sure we've resolved this issue. We need to keep you in the hospital until this infection and inflammation calm down. We've also done some blood work to make sure we have the full picture of what's going on and are still waiting for all the results. Do you have any questions?"

I didn't have any questions for him, but he went on to explain that most likely, I had a sexually transmitted disease that had started the whole thing, and the antibiotic should take care of that as well. He recommended that moving forward when considering sexual relations that I should insist that the man always uses a condom. He said I had to assume the responsibility of protecting myself in sexual encounters. He further explained that birth control pills were great for preventing pregnancy, but they offered no protection from sexually transmitted diseases.

The doctor's news left me feeling pretty depressed. I wasn't sure at all if I would ever be in a relationship. I could feel good enough about to actually consider having a couple of kids, but being told I most likely couldn't and wouldn't have any was discouraging. I was only nineteen years old.

Mrs. Sands offered to pick me up from the hospital, and she invited me to spend a few days with her family while I was recuperating. She was pretty sure I wouldn't receive any care from the guys at the townhouse, and I would be limited for a few days as a result of the surgery. I was released early in the afternoon the next day, and Mrs. Sands came to pick me up to take me back to her home. It was very nice of her, as I had no family close by I could call on in my circumstances. I enjoyed my time with her family. She was the one person in my life I did trust. As a caseworker, she had gone out on a limb for me trying to keep me out of trouble. She continued to be a help to me even after her responsibility for me had come to an end.

Chapter 12

He Loves Me, He Loves Me Not

While living at the townhouse, I met a guy named Dave. He was over six feet tall, had blonde hair and blue eyes, and was a nice-looking fellow, though not my normal type. He owned a motorcycle, and I happened to enjoy motorcycle rides. He also owned a car. He let me drive his car back and forth to work when he could drive his motorcycle. His mother had died when he was only three years old, but we never discussed the circumstances of her death. Unbeknown to me at the time, her death had caused a lot of unresolved problems for Dave. Very shortly after we met, we decided to move in together and share an apartment. He kept asking me to marry him, but I told him I didn't need a piece of paper from the government telling me it was okay to sleep with somebody.

Returning home from work one day, I picked up a hitchhiker. I had done a lot of hitchhiking in my time and had a soft spot for them and didn't realize how dangerous it could be. Anyway, I took a left turn and cut it too close and hit a car sitting at the traffic light waiting to turn. The hitchhiker started freaking out. "I've got quite a bit of pot on me. You need to leave, or we're both going to get busted," he said.

I panicked and, in a split second, left the scene of the accident. A couple of miles down the road, I let the hitchhiker out and headed home. I was very shaken up. I got pulled over on the way home, I think, for failure to use my signal, and as soon as the officer approached the car, I started blubbering that I didn't mean to leave. I explained that I had just panicked, so I was charged with hit and run, a very serious offense.

Through some friends, I found an attorney. I told Mr. Attorney what had happened, leaving out the details about my hitchhiker, and asked if he could help me. He said he would try to get the charges reduced, but he thought it would be helpful if I called the victims and apologized to them. The only good news is that I was going slowly, so no one in the car was injured, and we were just dealing with a personal property issue. They were really angry. Mr. Victim explained to me that they were on the way to take the car to trade it in for a new car when I hit them. He asked, "If you hit a dog, would you leave?"

"No, of course not," I said.

"So, in your eyes, the life of a dog is more valuable than my life and the life of my family members?" he asked angrily.

This was not going well at all. I apologized profusely and disconnected the call once it was apparent I wasn't getting anywhere.

In spite of the hostility of the victims, Mr. Attorney was able to get the charges reduced to "failure to maintain control of the vehicle," a much lesser charge.

On July 10, 1973, Mama McQuaide called me to tell me my father had died, and I shouldn't let the family keep me from going to the funeral if I wanted to go. I didn't think going to the funeral was a good idea because of having to deal with my mother. I hadn't seen her for quite some time, but I was sure if I showed up, uninvited, she would unleash her fury on me. There was no telling what she would do, and I saw it as an unnecessary risk. I had already endured enough abuse and didn't want any more. However, because I had many unresolved issues in my life involving my father, I was deeply saddened by the finality of his death. Now, I would never have an opportunity to talk to him about anything that had happened. I had never seen him again after running away in April 1969 and had looked forward to an opportunity to let him know just how much I hated him and how much loss I had suffered because of him. That was never going to happen now.

On November 3, 1973, I consented and married Dave, after knowing him for four months at the most, before a justice of the peace. I really didn't see the necessity of marriage, but it seemed important to him. Things seemed to go fine those first few months, though Dave's stepmother and father both had told me it was not a good idea to marry him. They said that he wasn't stable and had a bad history. They also told me he had been married before, and it hadn't ended well. I even ran into his ex-wife, and she had some interesting things to say, but Dave denied all of it.

Shortly after getting married, we traded in his car for a red Volkswagen Karmann Ghia. Dave taught me how to drive it because it was a manual shift instead of an automatic. I didn't take to it easily, and that car endured a lot of jerking and stalling out before I could manage the connection between the clutch and the gas pedal and smoothly change gears. I must say the man displayed amazing patience during what could have only been described as an ordeal for him. I finally got the hang of it, and I loved driving a standard. It was more fun, and I was more aware of the car. I was a little proud of myself, too, because I had actually stuck with something difficult until I got the hang of it.

I heard that the postal service was hiring, and I was able to get a much better paying job at the Merrifield Sectional Center Facility, working for the United States Postal Service. I worked both the 3:00 PM to midnight and 10:00 PM to 6:30 AM shifts while employed by them. Eventually, I was trained to process mail for all of the state of Virginia, having to know at least the first three numbers of the zip codes of every city in the state.

Dave and I hadn't been married any time at all when he expressed his desire to have a baby. I asked him if he was ready to quit smoking pot and taking drugs as well as greatly reduce the amount of alcohol he drank. He said no. I told him I wasn't going to bring a baby into an environment where drugs were the norm. I kept taking my birth control pills. In this situation, I was sure I was right, so I was very stubborn and unrelenting to his many appeals.

We went for long motorcycle rides. He was wonderful to talk to and listen to as long as he wasn't drinking. He was very laid back and calming to be around. That was until he picked up a bottle. Whenever he had more than a couple of beers to drink, he got quite mean. When I was working nights, he was playing cards with some neighbors and gambling. He was losing money on a weekly basis.

One night, I made beef stroganoff for dinner. Dave began to yell at me, telling me he had already told me he didn't like beef stroganoff and threw the plate, loaded with food, across the room. The dinner plate broke as it hit the dining room wall making a big mess on the wall and the floor. And he certainly was not cleaning it up. Another time, I came home from work and found him in our bed having sex with another girl. He cried and wept after he sent her off, and he promised it would never happen again. Another night he pointed a loaded rifle at me and told me to read erotic books to him. The honeymoon was over, so to speak. We were having some serious problems.

One evening when he had quite a bit to drink, Dave started hitting me and accusing me of sleeping with other guys. I hadn't previously demonstrated much in the way of morals, but now I was married. That meant I was having sex only with him; that was simple for me, and that was the truth. When that incident was over, he cried and promised it would never, ever happen again. He was so sincere and sweet when he wasn't drinking but drinking brought out the ugly side.

Over the next couple of months, I found out he was having sex with an acquaintance of ours who also lived in our apartment complex. We were not close friends, but we had smoked pot, drank beer, and played cards together. And, of course, Dave promised it would never happen again. He would quit playing cards over there when I was working nights, he told me.

After that, he beat me two more times. He had been drinking both times. I was beaten for the first fifteen years of my life by my angry, cruel parents. When I said, "I do," I hadn't agreed to this kind of treatment. After the last beating, I saw the doctor to make sure I didn't have a concussion as Dave had punched me in the head several times. I had a really bad headache that hung on and wouldn't go away. I had seen the same doctor after each incident, and now he told me, in no uncertain terms, that the next time Dave might kill me. He was pretty angry with me that I was still living with a man who had done these things to me.

"He's not going to change, Rita, so let go of your wishful thinking. Get out and do it now. You have the whole rest of your life ahead of you, and you can start over. If he really loved you, he wouldn't be hitting you. Period. Move out and do it now. I don't want to have to complete a death certificate for you, but that's how this will end if you don't walk away. Do you hear me?"

The doctor was right. I had a choice to make, and this was not going to be my future. Dave was not capable of changing without some professional help, which he wouldn't consider. I would have contemplated staying if he had shown a willingness to address the issues. I wasn't safe with him and his dramatic mood swings. He would be fine one minute and exploding in rage the next. I had nicknamed him Dr. Jekyll and Mr. Hyde during the last few months.

Also, of course, he didn't quit seeing Jan. He continued to play cards and drink and smoke pot with her and her roommates while I was working.

The next day, when he went to work, I called a friend I worked with at the post office and made arrangements to stay with her until I could figure out what to do. It was January 19, 1975. We had been together for a total of nineteen months, but I knew in my heart, I was done. This marriage was over. I loaded the front passenger seat and the backseat of the Karmann Ghia with my clothes and personal belongings. I left him a note on the coffee table, letting him know he had beaten me for the last time. "Three Strikes, You're Out!" it said. Then I left. I moved into the guest bedroom of my friend Karen's single-family home. She was a single mother with a darling little girl, Kristy. I was torn up emotionally because deep down I felt marriage was "until death do us part." I had taken a vow I didn't take lightly. I was filled with regret. Why had I let him talk me into marriage? Living together had been working for me. Why did I give in to marriage?

When I got to work the next day, I let my employers know I had a new temporary address and telephone number and then went about my normal duties of sorting mail. One great thing about that job was once I learned the basics of what was required, I could do a lot of thinking. I was pondering what I would do next, when I got paged to the office. I was told I had a telephone call.

"Hey, bitch," Dave greeted me. "Why don't you go out to the parking lot and see if you can find your car? And let me tell you, I am just getting started!" He hung up.

Sure enough, my car was missing from the parking lot. I made arrangements with Karen to run me by my former apartment, so I could pick up the car, but it wouldn't start because he had removed the distributor cap. I was furious! I went up to the apartment door and pounded on it. He opened the door with a self-righteous smirk on his face.

"If this is how you want to play this, you bastard, I will be back tomorrow with the payment book, and you can take over the payments on the car!" I yelled at him.

"You left without giving me any warning, you bitch!" he yelled back.

"You didn't deserve any warning, you prick! You beat the hell out of me. You're sleeping with our neighbor! I'm done! I'm filing for a divorce as soon as I have money for an attorney!"

This put him on the spot. He wouldn't have my money to help with rent and other expenses. The verbal volleying went on a bit longer, but then he reluctantly surrendered the extra key to the car and came down and put the distributor cap back on. I paid attention as I would be removing it myself when I had to go into work just in case he had another key I didn't know about. Also, he had seen who gave me a ride over, and it wasn't too hard for him to put two and two together and figure out where I was staying. Previously, I had talked about Karen, and he'd met her a time or two because she was a good friend.

A couple of weeks later, when I got back to Karen's house after getting off work, she said, "We need to talk."

"What's up?" I asked.

"I got a call today," she continued. "It was Dave, and he said if I don't put you out, he's going to shoot Kristy at the bus stop tomorrow morning!"

"The bastard!" I exclaimed, shaking my head.

"Rita, I am really sorry, but you're going to have to leave. I can't risk it, and I think he is just unstable enough that he might do it. He sounds like he's out of his mind!"

Of course I had to leave. Neither of us was willing to see if he would go through with his threat. I once again packed all my stuff into the car. This time I checked into a hotel that had weekly rates until I could figure out what to do next. I had been in the hotel for only about three days when there was a pounding on my door, which opened from the street right into my room. Dave was yelling and cussing and demanding to come in. I heard him through the door. He must have followed me here when I was leaving work one day. There was no other way he could know where I was staying. I ducked into the bathroom and locked the door, putting another door between us. I could hear sirens getting closer, so, mercifully, someone had called the police. It was enough to scare Dave off for the moment. I left the shelter of the bathroom when those identifying themselves as police knocked on my hotel door.

I explained to the officers that I had left Dave because he continued to phys-ically abuse me, and I was ending the relationship. I also told them he had threatened to shoot Kristy at the bus stop. They recommended that I come down to the police station and file a restraining order against him. I gave them his information, name, date of birth, address, and telephone number. They approached some other witnesses standing outside to talk with them. The management of the hotel came and told me that I would have to go; they couldn't allow their other guests to be endangered. Once again, I packed up my car and would have to find a new place to stay.

About four weeks after I left him, I was thoroughly convinced that I never wanted to deal with this lunatic again. He had stolen my car, threatened to kill an innocent child, and frightened and bullied me whenever I saw him or talked to him. He was more than capable of carrying out his threats, and he was unstable enough to do so. His father, stepmother, and ex-wife had all warned me that he was bad news, and unfortunately, I had to learn it the hard way!

I called and made an appointment with Mr. Attorney. As I drove to his of-fice, I thought it was pretty sobering that I was only twenty and already had a lawyer in my life. I was saddened by the mess things had become. I told the attorney about the three beatings, the threat against Kristy, and that Dave continued to terrorize me whenever he had the opportunity. Mr. Attorney said the easiest thing to do, since we had no children and no property, was to file for a divorce on the grounds of irreconcilable differences. He said it was new in Virginia, and the terms were a one-year legal separation with no sex between us during that year. He said it was straightforward and not too expensive. I signed the papers to make the legal separation effective the day I had left Dave and provided proof of all my residences since leav-ing him. Additionally, the lawyer recommended that I do as the police had suggested and sign a restraining order against Dave, which might bring a stop to his dangerous behavior. He said once I had filed it, he would be able to get a copy of the restraining order and submit it with all the other legal documentation.

I got word through the grapevine that Jan, the neighbor Dave had been sleeping with, needed to talk to me. Apparently, she was more than his card buddy because she was pregnant and assured me the baby was Dave's. She was hoping there would be no hard feelings. I told her what I thought of her for sleeping with a married man when there were lots of unmarried men who would have been happy to have sex with her.

This latest development was just icing on the cake. I wasn't surprised. I had caught him in bed with someone else while we were just living together. Marriage seemed to bring out the worst in him. I was pretty sure he had abandonment issues from his mother dying when he was so young.

Dave was going to get that baby he was after, and he would probably have his third wife by age twenty-five. Yeah, I had lost a good one! Well, this could be received as good news because now maybe he would stop harassing me. I might be able to really move on with my life without having to deal with him anymore.

Now that Dave was with Jan, I felt it was safe to go ahead and get my own place. I rented a one-bedroom apartment on the second floor of an apartment complex in Fairfax, Virginia. During the few months we had been separated, I had moved a minimum of eight times in six months because he would find out where I was staying and contact the people living there and threaten to burn their homes down and other charming things like that. I was looking forward to having a place of my own and the end to all the moving and running and hiding. I also finally had my own telephone number, which I gave to Dave, as he did need to get in touch with me sometimes, and I no longer felt threatened by him. I didn't, however, give him my address.

Thankfully, the apartment I had shared with him had been leased in Dave's name. My name was not on the lease. He had to stay there until the lease was up or forfeit his security deposit. He couldn't afford to do that. Jan also had a lease obligation, so until they could get their own place, Dave had gotten a roommate who was content to sleep on the couch until the lease was up. This helped offset his expenses.

Don't ask me how it happened, because I can't remember, but Dave's new roommate, Charlie and I had some kind of immediate chemistry, and we had started seeing each other. We were careful and tried to keep it from Dave because he was crazy and unpredictable. We usually just met at my apartment. I did let him know that I was not ready for him to move in, and it would not be a consideration at all until my divorce was final.

I called Dave to arrange a time for him to sign some paperwork for the Department of Motor Vehicles to take his name off the registration and title and paperwork for the bank, removing his name from the loan for the Karmann Ghia. I headed over to his place with the paperwork at the appointed time and knocked on the door. Dave let me in, acting friendly and normal, if not a little weird, and said he had to get something from the bedroom. He asked me if I wanted to join him and have a little fun. I couldn't believe he was asking me to have sex with him with all that he had put me through over the last several months. I let him know that sex between us would never happen again. He told me it was my loss and went to the bedroom.

He returned to the living room with his gun, a double-barreled sawed-off shotgun. Completely out of control, he called me a whore and a bitch, reminding me that I was still his wife. Who did I think I was giving what was rightfully his to another man? Interesting, coming from a man who got another woman pregnant while we were still married and living under the same roof. Apparently, word had gotten back to him that Charlie and I were seeing one another.

I had seen that gun before; he used to sit across from me and point it at me to intimidate me while he had me read to him from filthy books. I didn't even know if it was loaded during those times and figured it wasn't. He was drunk when he did this, and, as long as I humored him and read him the books, it never went beyond his pointing the gun at me. But this time, he assured me the gun was loaded while he continued to swear at me. He told me no court in the land would convict him for killing a whore like me, and that is surely what I was since I was sleeping with another man. He had the barrel pressed into my forehead. I was pretty sure I was going to die. He was beyond furious and jealous and crazy! It shut me up for a few minutes while he continued to rant and swear and call me names.

"You know I have every right to kill you! Admit it!" he continued to scream at me, pressing the gun more forcefully against my forehead.

Well, if I was going to die anyway, I was pretty sure the least I deserved was the last word. I used almost the same words I had used when I was threatened on the streets of Washington with a knife a few years back. The weapon and the perpetrator were the only things that had changed.

"Well, go ahead and shoot me! I'll be dead and actually free from ever having to deal with your sorry ass again. You won't be my problem any longer. You'll be the one with fingerprints on a gun and a dead body in your living room, not to mention the mess you're going to create in this room! Go ahead! Shoot me," I yelled at him.

Dave still hadn't removed the gun from my forehead. I started to tremble violently, and I wet my pants, pee running down the inside of my jeans and into my socks.

"I guess Jan might come to see you in prison and bring your baby with her if she's still in the picture," I blurted out.

At those words, Dave lowered the gun. I was so very grateful that his thoughts of the birth of his child just a few months away caused him to reconsider his actions and allowed me to continue to live. He was in a stupor and obviously quite shaken by what he had almost done. He turned and headed back to the bedroom with the gun, carrying it gingerly and with the barrels pointed toward the floor. I grabbed my purse and all my paperwork from the coffee table and fled the apartment. I locked the doors as soon as I was safely in my car. He was running out the front door towards me when I put the car in reverse and floored it, taking a few risks as I escaped the complex and his presence. I would ask Mr. Attorney to set up a time with Dave to go to his office to sign the paperwork. I had no intention of ever seeing him again unless it was in the safety of a law office or courtroom. And I didn't have to be there for him to sign the paperwork.

Chapter 13

Charlie

A few months after the gun incident, I went to Rockfish, North Carolina, with Charlie and met his family. His mother told me, "You can do way better than my son, honey. It pains me to say it, but he will bring you nothing but sorrow. Trouble follows him wherever he goes."

Late Friday night, Charlie said he wanted to go for a ride so he could show me some of Rockfish. It was late, and I wasn't sure how much I was going to see, but I agreed to his plan. After being in the car for just a few minutes, it was obvious this was more than just a ride around Rockfish. He was giving me very specific driving directions. He had me back the car up to a particular house and turn the car off. Charlie told me to be quiet and wait in the car. He just had to check something out, and it might take a few minutes.

It was almost thirty minutes later, and I was getting impatient trying to figure out what to do when he sidled up to the driver's window and asked me to pop the trunk. I popped the trunk release, and Charlie spent the next several minutes loading things in the trunk. Then he closed the trunk and jumped into the car. Dogs were barking all over the neighborhood.

"Let's get out of here," he said, unsuccessfully trying to sound nonchalant.

"What's all that stuff you put in the trunk?" I asked.

"I used to live here, and a friend was storing some stuff for me. He told me I couldn't leave it here anymore, so I was just picking up my things," he explained.

It didn't make sense to me. If it was a friend's house, why were we sneaking around in the dark, and why was there no sign of this friend? But I didn't question him further. Looking back, I should have questioned him a lot more.

When his mother had left to do some errands on Saturday morning, the mail came. There were several birthday cards for her. Charlie opened all of them and took the money out of her cards and put it in his wallet.

"She would want me to have this," he said, justifying himself. "Get your suitcase together, and let's get out of here."

When I got out of the car with my suitcase, he took it from me and put it in the backseat. Apparently, there was no room in the trunk. We then drove back to Fairfax. After we got back to my apartment, I made us something to eat. While I was cleaning up the table and kitchen, he went to the hall closet and was getting stuff out of jacket pockets. When I returned to the living room, he had something white and powdery in a baggie that he told me was cocaine; there was a needle lying on the coffee table.

"I don't have much," he said, "but it's plenty for both of us to get a nice high."

"I don't like needles," I informed him. "I haven't used them in years."

"Well, I know how to use them. The thing is, if you just snort it, you have to wait a while before you feel the high, but when you use a needle, the rush is immediate. I won't hurt you. I know what I'm doing."

I watched him prepare the powder with a little bit of water on a spoon and then draw the mixture up into the needle.

"Are you gonna try it?" he asked.

I turned my head away and let him inject it into my veins. He was right. The high was immediate, and it was wonderful. Cocaine was an amazing high; for the duration of the experience, everything was great, and there was a sense of peace. I had only had cocaine a few times before this incident. After that, I used it whenever the opportunity presented itself and got a dealer's name from him, so I could score some for myself when he wasn't around. Charlie left me the needle, though I was never able to inject it myself. If he wasn't around, I would just snort it. The high wasn't immediate and not as powerful, but it was still a decent high.

When it was quite dark outside, Charlie said, "I need you to help me empty out the trunk. I just want to leave some stuff here for a couple of weeks. I can't take it to Dave's place. I'm not sure how much longer I'll be staying with him."

We both went out to the car. There were a couple of floor lamps and a few boxes. We unloaded the trunk and stored it all in a corner of my living room. On closer inspection, I saw that the floor lamps were beautiful and looked quite old. There was also a decanter made from etched glass with four matching hot beverage cups. The set was beautiful. Charlie said it was Russian, and it looked very valuable to my untrained eye. There were some other unique and beautiful things, but I can't remember details, only that my trunk had been filled with what appeared to be antiques. The floor lamps had a little piece of string tied around one of the arms and a tag with a price on it.

"Where did you get this stuff?" I asked again, beginning to wonder what I had just allowed him to unload into my apartment.

"I told you, it's some stuff a friend stored for me, and I don't have anywhere else I can keep it right now. I'll have it out of here in two weeks tops," he responded.

He kissed me and left for the couch at Dave's. I had to be at work early the next day, and we had an understanding as I really didn't like overnight company when I had to get up early.

When I got back to my apartment after work and was confronted with the collection of boxes and lamps and valuables Charlie had stored in my living room, I started wondering. What if it was stolen? Where else would he get things that looked so expensive? The pieces had price tags on them, and he had retrieved them in the dark. And he had stolen money from his own mother, after all.

How much did I know about this guy? Not much, but even his mother said he was trouble. Maybe I should give some consideration to what she said. I hadn't listened to Dave's father and stepmother, and I could have avoided the multiple abuses I experienced as his wife if I had taken heed to their words.

Charlie didn't visit over the next several days, and I had to do something. If this was stolen goods and it was found in my apartment, I could get into some serious trouble. The more I thought about it, the more convinced I was that it was stolen. I called the non-emergency number of the police department and asked if an officer could call me or stop by. The dispatcher wanted me to tell her why, and I asked to just have an officer call me, and I would explain when they called. The dispatcher asked me if I was in any danger, and I told her no.

An officer did call a few minutes later, and I explained that my boyfriend of just two or three months had asked to store some stuff in my apartment, and I was suspicious about what it was and where he had gotten it. I told him things just didn't seem normal. I asked the officer what I should do. He offered to send over a couple of officers to take a look; then they would decide what should be done. He asked if I would be home for a while because he could send someone fairly soon. I told him I would stay home until they came, and he advised me what I needed to do.

After a while, two uniformed officers showed up at my place. They looked at the items and said they were pretty sure it was all stolen, so they were going to take it in as evidence and do some research. They asked me if I had any idea where Charlie had gotten the pieces. I told them about our trip to Rockfish to see his family and that Charlie had borrowed my car for an errand. I didn't incriminate myself; after all, I hadn't stolen it. I told them when I had asked him about the stuff, he said it was all his, and he could no longer store it at his friend's home in North Carolina. They asked me a few more questions, mostly about Charlie. I told them I had been dating him only for a short time and really knew very little about him, but his stories were starting to sound pretty suspicious. The officers took Charlie's contact information, and I also told them where he worked. While they waited, I wrote out a statement for their records of everything I had told them. They told me they would be in touch if they needed additional information and also left a business card should I remember anything else they might need to know regarding the suspicious property.

Charlie showed up a couple of days later, and I told him some uniformed officers came over to talk to me about some particulars with the restraining order against Dave and that we had been talking in the living room. I told him they took an interest in all the stuff he had stored there, and they took it all when they left.

"Oh, shit," he said. "What did you tell them?"

"I told them exactly what you told me. You retrieved some of your belong-ings from a friend in North Carolina who had been storing it for you, and you had no place to keep it and asked to store it at my place for a couple of weeks," I said.

"Did you give them my name?" he asked in a panic.

"Of course, I did," I responded. "Why shouldn't I? It's not like it was stolen or anything. It was just a matter of storage, right?" What could he say to me? That was exactly what he had told me.

"Oh, shit! Why didn't you make something up to tell them?" he angrily asked.

"Why would I need to make something up if you told me the truth?" I asked, just as angrily.

"I'm going to have to leave town for a while," Charlie said. "I'll be in touch when I make it back to the area. If you need to get a hold of me, you can leave a message with my mother. Leave a message for sure if the cops call or show up and it has to do with the stuff, okay?" he asked, handing me a slip of paper with his mother's telephone number on it. He didn't even kiss me before he left; he was visibly shaken.

"Wow," I said to myself out loud after he was gone, "you're dodging bullets right and left. You need to pay more attention to what's going on around you before you get your ass locked up for someone else's bullshit!"

Not seeing him for a while would be a good thing. I had gotten into that relationship while still reeling from the insanity with Dave. Maybe this was why rebounding was just not a great idea. I wasn't seeing things that were right before me! It was dangerous to live on autopilot. And as I got to think-ing about it, Charlie didn't beat me or anything, so far, but he was not much of an improvement over Dave. I was pretty sure he lied to me all the time, telling me what he thought I wanted to hear.

I worked forty hours a week at the post office and overtime when it was offered. Handling hundreds of pieces of mail a day kept my mind off the unrest and turmoil I felt inside when I had a free minute to think. When I wasn't working, I was smoking pot and snorting coke weekly and not feel-ing much of anything. Between sorting the mail and drugs, I kept myself pretty numb. That is the best I could do to get through life. The overwhelming pain floating below the surface had to be subdued at all costs. There really was no telling what would happen if it rose to the surface in full force. I was terrified of something happening one day, some little insignificant something that would be the proverbial straw that broke the camel's back, and I would end up some place in my mind from which there would, or could, be no return. That is what I feared.

Chapter 14

More Bad Choices

Winston, a good friend and my source for pot, told me he was a little hot and asked if he could stash some pot at my house just until things settled down. He thought it would be two weeks at the longest. I said sure and had about ten pounds of his pot at my house divided into several gallon-size storage bags. I had a brass, tiered plant stand in my living room and I put all his pot on the middle shelf of that stand.

At the time, I was working the 10:00 PM to 6:30 AM shift at the post office. I got home from work on this particular morning and ate a snack before going to bed. Most of the time, I didn't go to bed until later in the day, but I was feeling exhausted. I woke up to someone pounding on my apartment door. I slipped on one of my long tee shirts and a pair of pajama bottoms. Glancing at my alarm clock, I saw it was about 2:30 PM I went to see who was at the door. Through the peephole, I could see two uniformed police officers.

"Yes?" I said through the closed door.

"Are you Rita Ann Roth?" one of the officers asked.

"Yes," I replied.

"We need to talk with you, and it's probably in your best interest if we talk inside," one of them replied.

I opened the door and ushered them into the living room.

"We have a warrant for your arrest for contempt of court. You missed a court appearance scheduled for this morning in Petersburg, Virginia," one of the officers explained.

"Apparently, you got a speeding ticket in Petersburg, and they had not received payment for the fine by mail. If they don't have payment before your court date, you have to be in court to explain why," the officer continued when he saw my puzzled expression.

"I did get a speeding ticket when I went to visit my grandmother, but I did pay the fine," I said. "I mailed in a postal money order a few days ago. Give me a second, and I'll find the receipt for my payment."

"Unfortunately, miss, you'll have to tell that to the magistrate. We have to serve the warrant, which means we have to take you in. Bring your receipt with you, and you can work it out with the magistrate," he said.

"Well, I have to get dressed," I said. "My bedroom is back here. You don't have to worry. I'm not going anywhere. This is a pain in my ass after working all night because I should be sleeping as I have to work all night again tonight. Let me just get some clothes on."

One of the officers walked past me, going into the bedroom. He pulled open the curtain that led to the balcony two floors up. I guess he agreed that I wasn't going anywhere because he exited the room, pulling the bedroom door closed, but he let me know they were waiting right in the next room.

I was pulling my jeans on when I remembered all the pot in the living room, the room where they were waiting for me. Oh, my God, I thought. They're probably sitting on the couch, right across from the pot, looking right at it. It was not hidden. I wasn't expecting to have cops in my apartment at all, so it had seemed a reasonable place to store it at the time.

I could just see it now....

Oh, silly officer, I imagined myself saying, that's not my pot; it belongs to a friend of mine, and I'm just storing it for him until your department loses interest in him.

Yeah, that was not going to fly! I couldn't believe how stupid I had been. And I was just sure Winston would say, "Yeah, arrest me, not her. It's mine!"

"Be right out," I hollered from the bedroom.

I came out of the bedroom with my purse over my shoulder, dressed and ready to go and trying really hard not to stare at the shelf with the pot on it. Maybe some type of miracle had occurred, and, in a moment of clarity, I actually had stored the pot in the coat closet, out of sight, then promptly forgotten what I had done. The urge to look at the shelf was so strong. I almost gave in, but surely their eyes would follow my eyes. That's how it always happened on television anyway.

The two officers were sitting on my couch right across from the pot; it was at just about eye level for them. But they were engaged in a conversation that didn't seem to have anything to do with a potential drug bust.

Don't look at it, you idiot, I was screaming at myself in my head. Breathe, breathe, the silent self-talk continued. Act normal; don't act suspiciously!

"Let me just check here in the dining room for my money order receipt," I said, walking past them into the adjoining room. I flipped through some papers on the dining room table.

"Here it is," I said, holding it up victoriously. "Made out to the City of Petersburg for $125.00, and the ticket number is even on here as a reference," I said, waving it in front of them.

"Again, we don't have the authority to absolve you," one of the officers explained. "The magistrate has to do that."

As we were driving to the station, I remembered my purse had my rosewood pipe in it and a film vial full of pot. And this same purse was now riding in a police cruiser and heading for a police station. I was just having a day fraught with adventure and stupidity!

When we arrived at the station, I told the officers I really needed to use the lady's bathroom. One of the officers escorted me to the bathroom and obviously intended to wait for me outside the door. My heart was racing like crazy. Once in the lady's room, I turned the water on to make noise and opened my purse and took out the pipe and film vial and dropped them in the metal waste bin right under the paper towel dispenser, which was a one-piece unit. I flushed one of the toilets so as not to arouse suspicion regarding my real motive for using the restroom.

I left the restroom and was taken to a holding room to await the magistrate. I finally saw the magistrate, and he looked my receipt over. He advised me to mail my money in a little sooner next time to avoid this type of inconvenience for everyone. One of the officers pointed out a telephone, so I could call for a ride home. I called my friend Joe, and he said he could pick me up in about thirty minutes and give me a ride back to my place. I almost never left home without a good book to read, but with all the stress I had endured leading up to getting to the station, a book hadn't even entered my mind.

I went back to the lady's room and retrieved my favorite rosewood pot pipe and my film vial from the trash can. This adventure had cost me hours of sleep; no sense in losing my favorite pipe too! As Joe and I were driving to my place, I told him what had happened and about stashing the pot for someone.

"You have got to get that out of there immediately," he said. "Since they were there regarding a traffic issue, I don't think they could have done anything about the weed even if they saw it. They would have to go back to the magistrate and ask for another warrant, I think."

As we pulled into my parking lot, I looked for any unfamiliar cars. I was on high alert and would not have been surprised to find an unmarked car in my lot, keeping an eye on things. I didn't see anything and breathed a sigh of relief.

"What?" Joe asked.

"I was pretty much expecting maybe an unmarked car in here with an undercover guy keeping an eye on the comings and goings," I confessed. "I am really glad no one is here! I have time to get rid of something I should have never taken in the first place! Sometimes I surprise myself. I obviously didn't think this one through."

"Rita, to be honest with you, Karen and I have been pretty worried about you," Joe said. "I know this impending divorce and the crazy stunts Dave has pulled over the last several months have put you under a tremendous amount of stress, but you have got to do something. You've made some thoughtless decisions here lately that could have had very serious ramifications. Like getting yourself locked up! You have got to snap out of it! Aren't you concerned about the number of close calls you've had lately? I'm here for you if you need anything. You know that. But you need to be here for yourself. It's as if you're really just not aware of what's really happening around you and what you're allowing to happen. Are you doing anything else besides smoking pot? Cocaine? Acid?" he asked.

"Mostly just pot," I answered. "Cocaine here and there." No need to confess to him that I was smoking pot every day. I had stopped smoking it on my lunch break when I was working because it made me too sleepy, but I smoked a couple of bowls in my rosewood pipe after work and before bed, and it helped me sleep.

"That's good," he said. "You don't need drugs confusing things right now, so keep it that way, okay?"

Joe was sort of like the big brother I never had. I knew he was right! It didn't surprise me that he and Karen had discussed my situation. They had been close friends long before I had arrived on the scene.

In the process of shutting down emotions so I wouldn't feel painful things deep, deep inside, a few other switches had got flipped off as well. They were switches that needed to be on all the time. All the pain with Dave over the last several months had stirred up reservoirs of unresolved junk swirling beneath the surface and screaming to be heard. I had no intention of listening to or looking at any of it. Where would I even start? Where would I end up? It was truly terrifying! I really wasn't that stupid, which is what made my current state so bad. I was not paying attention, and that is stupid if it lands you in big trouble.

I called Winston as soon as I got inside and told him we needed to meet. I explained about the cops who had been in my apartment and who could have seen the pot. I insisted it had to be moved immediately. We met in the back of a large strip mall parking lot, and I gave him his pot back. I determined I would never store drugs for a friend again! I felt a tremendous weight lift after I had gotten the pot out of my apartment. I hadn't realized how much extra stress that quantities of pot in one's possession could cause.

I loved Karen, and she had enough on her plate without worrying about me, too. I gave her a call and told her I was "awake" now, and she didn't need to worry about me anymore.

"What is it with you and men?" she asked.

"What do you mean?" I asked.

"You've ended up with some real winners!" she replied. "I know the stuff with your father is not resolved, and it seems like it is seriously clouding your judgment when it comes to guys. You've been in some dangerous situations that most people never deal with in their lives. I'm worried about you and the choices you're making. I have the name of a very good therapist if you need to talk to someone. It's her job to help you get some messed-up things straightened out. She's helped me a lot."

"Let me think about it," I said, not making any promises. "How's Kristy doing in school?" I asked, changing the subject.

After getting off the phone with Karen, I determined to steer clear of relationships with men for a while. It was too complicated, and I didn't need complications right now. I needed a break from complications.

I received my divorce papers in the mail on Friday, March 26, 1976, from Mr. Attorney, just over a year after filing for the divorce. I was oddly saddened when I opened the mail and saw what the envelope contained. I didn't regret my decision to leave him; it was the right choice. I regretted marrying him in the first place, which put me in a position, just a short time later, to divorce him. I had married him, believing marriage is "until death do us part." I don't know if that was residual from my Catholic upbringing or due to all the fairy tales I read. Maybe there was a little bit of hope left in me despite the many things I had endured.

Dave, waiting in the wings to marry Jan, hadn't contested it as he had originally threatened. In addition to citing irreconcilable differences as the reason for the divorce, Mr. Attorney had listed the abuse, physical and mental, and included that I had to take out a restraining order because of his threats and actions against me. Mr. Attorney had my maiden name, Roth, restored, and I was legally free of Dave. I was so glad I had no children with him, which would have tied me to him for years to come.

After the divorce was finalized, I went through a few months of serious drinking. I was drinking things that tasted so good and harmless that I had a hard time perceiving the volume of the alcohol in the drinks. It took me a while to realize I didn't have much of a threshold at all. I liked White Russians, but I was also trying to develop a taste for Scotch on the rocks with a twist of lime. I actually thought the Scotch was a wiser choice. The alcohol wasn't hidden and wasn't blended with other yummy ingredients, so I was less likely to overdo it.

I'm not really sure why I turned to drinking. Like pot, it numbed the pain I felt inside, but I never lost control with pot. I seemed to always be losing control with alcohol. I didn't lose my memory with pot. When drinking, I had many occasions when I couldn't remember things that had happened. Over the next several months, I had a couple of incidents where I had been drinking and would wake up somewhere I didn't remember going. Often, I found myself in the home of total strangers. I was experiencing complete blackouts. It was really frightening, but that didn't stop me from drinking.

During this period of many bad choices, I also received several disciplinary actions from my supervisor at the post office. I wasn't showing up when scheduled and not calling ahead to let him know I was going to be late or not make it at all. When I realized I was probably on the verge of getting fired, I turned in my two weeks' notice. It was years later before I realized that my lack of self-control with alcohol had cost me a good job, one that paid well and had good benefits with no college degree required.

Charlie called me out of the blue from North Carolina to tell me he was moving to Florida to get a fresh start. He said he would be staying with a brother there until he could get on his feet, and he wanted to know if I wanted to go with him. I told him I wasn't in a place to consider a major relocation, when the truth was, I didn't want to be dependent upon him for anything.

I worked as a waitress in several mediocre restaurants before landing a job at a wonderful new restaurant in Annandale. The food they served was excellent, and I didn't have to look through the glasses for several minutes to be sure I wasn't offering water to the guests in something not properly cleaned. The restaurant was owned by three men who were all obviously happily married to their wives. They didn't assume that sex with the staff was one of the benefits they got for giving us a job. That attitude had been prevalent among the managers in a lot of restaurants where I had previously worked.

Unfortunately, they allowed us to drink at the bar after we got off work. One evening I was sitting at the bar drinking shots of tequila, vodka, and orange juice with some cute guy, and I lost all recollection of everything that happened after my third drink. I woke up in a hospital room alone -- I don't know how much later -- strapped to a hospital gurney. My head was absolutely pounding, and I had wet myself. I smelled terrible and couldn't begin to imagine what I looked like.

The doctor eventually came in to talk with me, and he was very angry.

"You have a problem, Miss Roth," he said to me. "You have severe alcohol poisoning, and, if you had had one more drink, you probably would have died. You need to get some professional help."

He gave me some forms to sign, then signed a release from the hospital, giving me a copy of the discharge papers to take with me. He also provided some telephone numbers I could call to see about getting some professional help. A nurse led me to the lobby. There were two uniformed police officers waiting for me.

"Rita Ann Roth?" one of them asked as they walked towards me.

"Yes," I replied.

"You are under arrest for being drunk in public, disturbing the peace, and assaulting a police officer," he said, putting handcuffs on me. They read me my rights, put me in the back of the squad car, and took me to the station. I remembered nothing. What in the world had I done? No details were forthcoming from these guys. I was still suffering from the consequences of having all that alcohol in my bloodstream, or I would have probably been asking them questions. I was allowed to make a phone call, and Joe came to the rescue once again. I was released into his custody. I had told him to bring a towel for me to sit on so I wouldn't mess up his car. Talk about embarrassing.

The next day I was scheduled to work a double at the restaurant from 11:00 AM to 2:00 PM and 5:00 PM to closing. I had to work a double with the worst hangover I had ever had in my life. I asked one of the other waitresses who had worked with me the night before what had happened when I got off. She told me I didn't want to know and wouldn't talk about it.

When I finished closing out my section for the night, Mike, one of the owners, approached me and told me he was sorry, but they were going to have to let me go after what had happened last night. He wouldn't give me any details either. He did say they were changing their policy, and employees wouldn't be allowed to drink on the premises anymore. I was totally depressed by this news, as they had been a really great group to work with, which was hard to find in the restaurant world. I had never been fired before! He said they would give me good references and say they had accepted my resignation. I would have to get out and find another job as soon as possible, but my immediate goal was to go home and take something for my splitting headache and get some sleep.

The drinking finally ended one night when I was arrested for driving while intoxicated. I had to spend the night in jail, and Karen came to get me the next day when I had been released. Fortunately, there was no car accident involved, and I hadn't hurt anyone, but I certainly shouldn't have been driving. I had gotten so many points against my license over the last year, and now there was a DWI; on top of that, my license was suspended, and I had a pretty substantial fine to pay. It would cost me a fortune to get my insurance reinstated. Losing my license made getting to the bar a bit more complicated. Drinking alone at home didn't appeal to me. I finally had a reason to quit drinking.

At this point, I had really messed up everything. I had no job and now had lost the ability to get out and find a new position because I couldn't drive myself anywhere. I was up the creek without a paddle, and I saw no options for changing my circumstances.

Chapter 15

The Worst Summer Ever

Without a job and unable to drive, Charlie's invitation to go to Florida with him seemed like my only option. So, I called his mother's house in North Carolina to see if he was still there. He answered the phone, and I asked him if he was still moving to Florida. He replied that he was. I asked him if the invitation was still open for me to go with him, and he said yes. I told him I had lost my license and asked him how I would get back and forth to work. He told me we really couldn't work things out until we were actually in Florida, but we would find a way to do what we needed to do. I still owned a car, and between him and his brother, they would get me to work once I found a job.

It seemed like the only solution to my problems. I could find new work and start over. Charlie said there was plenty of work in the area where we were moving, and he was sure I would have no trouble finding a job.

Let me just say that my summer in Florida is not among my favorite memories. We ended up staying in an apartment with Charlie's brother. His sister and infant twin daughters even stayed there for a while. No one had a normal job, and it didn't take me long to realize they were probably doing illegal things on a regular basis.

There was minimal food in the house, and if I was going to eat, I was going to have to find a job. I found a waitressing job and started bringing in a little money. I ate so many bologna and cheese sandwiches that summer that I absolutely cannot stand bologna to this day.

Cindy, Charlie's sister, would leave the girls in the apartment, sometimes when they were sleeping, and go out. I was completely appalled and horrified. How could someone who had been given such a gift neglect that gift so horribly? She was not the warm, lovey type and spoke sharply and abruptly to them throughout the day. I felt very sorry for the girls.

The others had pot and cocaine available on a regular basis and shared with me generously as I was keeping food in the refrigerator. I was letting Charlie shoot me up two or three times a week. He would shoot himself up first and then shoot me up. Cocaine made me feel as if everything really would be okay, at least during the time the drug was in my system. As it wore off, it was back to life as usual -- which was not so great. It was like "peace" coming into my bloodstream through that needle.

One-time Charlie shot me up with heroin instead of cocaine, but he didn't tell me it was heroin. I knew immediately something was wrong.

"What was in that syringe?" I demanded.

"It's heroin. You'll like it," he said.

He was wrong. I didn't like it at all. Coke provided an incredible high and feelings of euphoria; it was an upper. With heroin, I was very "down," and I didn't care for the feeling at all. I had to wait for hours for the effects to wear off. I had some choice words with Charlie over the incident. I was pissed.

"You would never have known if you liked it if you didn't try it. Take it easy," he said. "It's not that big of a deal."

"You had no right to give me heroin without my permission! You might like it, but I don't like it at all," I retorted. "I have never wanted to try it. It's a downer. I like to be up! Don't you ever do something like that to me again! Not your decision to make!"

I didn't like threatening him because he and his brother were starting to scare me. There was no telling what they might do if they felt too threatened. Both of them had been in and out of prison, and I was pretty sure I didn't know half of what was behind their convictions. Charlie assured me it wouldn't happen again, so I finally let the subject drop. However, this is when I started thinking I might need to get back to the Northern Virginia area. I was beginning to understand that I was in a very toxic situation from which I needed to extricate myself. I had no idea what they did during the day while I was working, and I didn't want to get in trouble because of whatever they were up to.

Charlie's brother didn't get it that I was with Charlie. One morning, I was still lying in bed on my side, with my face to the wall, when he dropped down behind me on the mattress. He moved his body close to mine and started kissing the back of my neck. I thought it was Charlie and rolled over in the bed after a couple of minutes and saw that it was his brother. I was horrified, disgusted, and infuriated. I told him his advances were not appreciated or welcome, to get out of my bedroom, and not to ever come in there again.

Who did these guys think they were, giving someone heroin when they thought it was cocaine and thinking someone was available for sex because they lived under the same roof? I was pretty sure complaining to Charlie would have gotten me nowhere. Again, I had to stand up for myself against men. The brother backed off, but I didn't trust him and was wary and on guard all the time.

One day I got dropped off at home by a coworker early as I wasn't feeling well. I found Charlie in our bed with a girl who looked no older than fifteen. I made sure he knew I had seen them before slamming the door and leaving the apartment. When we talked, several hours later, Charlie let me know that we weren't married, and he could sleep with others and so could I. He had made me no promise of a monogamous commitment. I had no intention of sharing his bed again. Married or not, we had been living together, and I didn't accept his terms. I started sleeping on the couch in the living room after the television was turned off and everyone had gone to bed.

I lay awake long after the lights were turned out, trying to determine my next move. I would be leaving Florida as soon as I came up with some type of plan.

The next day I called Karen and asked if I could stay with her just until I figured out my next move and told her I was in a toxic environment and just had to get out of there before things escalated any more. She agreed now that Dave was no longer stalking me.

I worked over the next three days, and sold my car to a coworker who paid me cash. At the end of my shift on Friday, I told the manager I wouldn't be coming back, that an emergency family situation required me to be away for an indefinite period of time. I apologized for not being able to give them more notice, but such was the nature of emergencies.

When I got back to the apartment that evening, I was told that Cindy and the girls had left for North Carolina for a visit with her mother for a few days. The guys were planning on going out for breakfast in the morning and asked if I would join them. I told them I was exceptionally tired and would prefer to sleep in. I lied to them, telling them the next day I was scheduled to work a lunch shift and then 4:00 PM to close. It sounded as if I would be able to make my escape without any extra drama.

I pretended to be asleep when Charlie and his brother left for breakfast the next morning. As soon as the apartment door closed, I was up and phoned the cab company to have a cab pick me up in thirty minutes. I took a quick shower and got dressed. Then I quickly packed my few belongings into my one suitcase.

For the second time in my life, I left a man by writing him a note on my way out the door. I was unable to face him and tell him what was going on because I had no idea what type of reaction there would be or if I could make a safe break because of the dynamics in that messed up, broken household.

In the note, I explained that I was needed elsewhere due to a family emergency, and I said I wouldn't be coming back. My postscript said, "I made no promises either."

I left the note on the dresser in Charlie's bedroom and didn't leave any forwarding address or contact information. I gave him no notice because I had finally realized I couldn't trust him. Were all my relationships with men destined to end with a note?

The taxi ride to the airport was uneventful. I paid my fare and gave the driver a good tip. I went into the airport and purchased my one-way ticket. I called Karen from a payphone and told her what time I expected my flight to arrive at the airport. She said either she or Joe would pick me up.

Karen picked me up at the airport. She told me not to worry about finding another place to live immediately. She said she had been skeptical at first about my moving back in as Dave had scared her so badly with that phone call she had received from him several months back threatening Kristy. She said I could take a little more time and maybe find something that would be more permanent for me.

Within a couple of weeks, I had even more issues to deal with. I was starting to feel pretty sick, and when I had a bowel movement, my stools had turned white. I was fatigued and had joint pain. I talked to Karen about it, and she told me I looked yellow. The whites of my eyes and my skin both looked yellow—even to me.

I made an appointment and went to the doctor. The doctor was pretty sure, from the symptoms I described and my appearance, that I had hepatitis, and the blood work he had done would most likely confirm it. I asked him how I got it. He wasn't oblivious to the tracks on my arms from my summer with Charlie. He told me sharing a needle with someone who was already a carrier or having sex with them was a sure way to end up being infected. He asked me if that was a possibility. I told him, after all the other things I learned about this person, I would not be surprised at all if he had hepatitis. I affirmed that he was the only one with whom I had shared a needle, but I had to acknowledge that I didn't know if he was a carrier.

The doctor gave me a prescription for some antiviral medicine and told me what to expect. He said I wouldn't be able to donate blood anymore. He also told me if I was still shooting drugs, he could recommend a great rehab program. I assured him I had stopped shooting drugs, and he told me to call back on Monday to get the results of the lab work and let him know how my body was responding to the medication. I would also need to make a follow-up appointment to have more blood work done to make sure things were improving.

In that moment, I felt like my life would never improve. Even the blood that flowed through my veins had been poisoned because of having shared my life, my body, and a needle with Charlie.

Chapter 16

Positive Changes

I found out from Karen that a couple, working the 10:00 PM to 6:30 AM shift at the post office, needed someone to be at their home overnight to keep an eye on their little girl, Mae. I had known Billy and his wife Tina, when I had worked at the post office. So, I called and asked them if they were still looking for a babysitter. They were still in need of someone, so Tina invited me to have dinner with them that night. I told her I didn't have a car, and she offered to pick me up at Karen's house. We would discuss some options, and I would meet their daughter.

Mae was a friendly little girl, around a year old, and I could tell we weren't going to have any problems getting along. Billy and Tina offered me room and board in exchange for being with Mae overnight. They showed me a room that would more than meet my needs. Tina generally made dinner every evening, and they ate around 6:00 PM. Everyone was on their own for breakfast and lunches, but if I let her know what I liked to eat, she would be sure it was available. They lived right off the major bus route in Falls Church. We discussed some of the details, and Tina told me to make sure I asked questions if she had not covered everything. Mae was to be my responsibility from 9:00 PM to 7:00 AM, the following day, on the nights they worked. When I was not taking care of Mae, my time was mine to do with as I saw fit. I could use the telephone and provide their number to my friends, but I would need to pay for any long distance calls I made.

I moved in the following weekend, and we all got along well. My "job" was not hard, as the little darling was easy to care for since she truly was sleeping almost the whole time. Tina put her down for bed before they left for work and bathed her when necessary. Initially, I was home during the day and would let Billy and Tina get a few hours of sleep while I fed, changed, and amused Mae.

I knew this was a temporary situation at best. My room and board were taken care of, but I had no income. I had to start thinking about the big picture. I had been living my life without goals or plans which could give me some type of direction and something to work towards. I was considering various options for how to provide for myself. I called Northern Virginia Community College to see about getting into their nursing program and was told there was a two-year waiting list. That was not going to work. I didn't have two years to wait to get started on something that could help to turn my life around.

One afternoon, I was watching television, and a commercial came on for the Washington School for Secretaries. They offered a nine-month secretarial program. There would be a reasonable expectation for those who finished the program of finding a well-paying job with benefits. That sounded pretty good to me, so I jotted the telephone number down and called the school. Secretarial instruction sounded like just the kind of training that might open new doors for me.

The next day, I took the bus into Washington, D.C. and filled out the application and applied for a student loan. Tina had loaned me a nice skirt, blouse, and shoes for the trip as I had jeans and nothing else. I met with someone in the business office to discuss my goals and told them it sounded like a good program that could provide stable employment when the training was complete. I said I was tired of waitressing as I had to always work nights and weekends to make decent money, and there were no benefits. I was quite pleased when I was told I was accepted and could start my training in a couple of weeks.

I had very low income at this point, so I was provided money with the student loan, around sixty-eight dollars if I remember correctly, by check each month to help out with expenses. The student loan I took out would cover the tuition and my books. Tina had a few outfits she gave me to wear to school as the dress code was professional and required dresses and skirts only.

I got a job at the Pizza Hut not too far from the house and worked just enough weekend hours to earn enough money to cover bus fare, cigarettes, pantyhose, and typing paper. Billy or Tina dropped me off and a coworker would take me home. One of the waiters had "Darth Vader" on his name tag, so I put "R2 D2" on my name tag. Most of the people there were fairly easy to get along with except the married manager who kept suggesting we have sex together. I suggested that maybe I should call his wife and tell her he was being perverted, disgusting, and unfaithful. He didn't fire me; I guess because I did my job well. Additionally, the customers and other staff liked me, and I had a good attendance record. I didn't quit because I needed the money and the restaurant was close to home. I basically started ignoring his lewd suggestions and didn't give him the satisfaction of any response.

Now, I was in school for the first time because I wanted to be, and I really saw it as an opportunity to get my life turned around. However, I had never done well socially in school because of all the issues in my life. Academically, I had initially striven to do my best as a young student. When no acknowledgment was forthcoming from either of my parents, I quit doing my best and became an average student who really struggled with math. When I was a child, we rarely lived anywhere long enough for me to make friends in school. Once I had hit the foster homes and was no longer under my mother's roof, I was not an easy person to be around. I was angry and had a bad attitude. I was the kind of kid other mothers would probably not encourage their children to befriend. In high school, I was the type of person who hung out with the other kids who didn't fit in.

I wasn't in this new environment for very long before I knew some of these gossipy girls were talking about me and making fun of my extremely limited wardrobe. I also caught on to who was doing most of the talking. Most of these kids obviously came from wealthy families and would not know what it meant to go without a meal. Everything they needed was provided for them and always had been. I resented their judgments when they knew nothing about me.

The school had an area where we were allowed to congregate for a cigarette break between classes. I approached the smoking lounge when those who had been doing the talking and making the snide remarks were all sitting having cigarettes. All talking ceased as soon as I sat down, and all eyes were on me.

"I really don't appreciate being talked about and criticized for my wardrobe," I began. "Let me just lay it out for you. I ran away from home when I was fifteen years old because my parents beat the hell out of me on a regular basis, and then I went through three foster homes. No one takes care of me, or helps me, or buys me the things I might need. I am what is called poor. I don't come from a well-to-do family, unlike most of you. So, it's really pretty rotten of you to talk about me. Do you think I like wearing the same outfits over and over? It's all I have, and someone gave me these things. Some of you have never worn the same outfit twice since I've been here, so how about you go searching through your closet and bring me the stuff you don't wear anymore? I wear a size ten. And quit talking about me! I'm doing the best I can with what I have, and I'm trying to turn my life around. I don't want your pity. I want you to stop bad-mouthing me."

Not really having had the liberty to talk or even to defend myself for the first fifteen years of my life had produced in me a desire to be heard and a need to explain myself. This resulted in direct and frank communication on my part. This was new to me, and I liked it. I knew it might not change anything, but these people would know I knew about the gossip and how I felt about it.

I remember their eyes were huge the whole time I confronted them. Some of them had begun to protest initially that they were not talking about me, but I ignored them and talked over them. I had no idea how my talk would affect them, but I just felt like the situation had to be addressed. The next day, three of those girls came to school with bags of clothes, just my size. I liked everything I was given. I enjoyed wearing my "new clothes," and I now had a lot more variety from which to choose. I was amazed at their generosity as I was given some very nice clothing. I also made several new friends with that group of girls. It was a turning point at school for me.

Besides the social aspect, I enjoyed the classes and studying. I was already a good speller because I loved reading. We were learning business and legal terms and how to use different office machines. Shorthand was a huge undertaking, but I loved it and exceeded the requirements of the class, taking 120 words a minute when only 100 words a minute were required. I did several hours of shorthand homework every night.

We also attended a personal development class where we discussed manners and protocol in the workplace and how we should carry ourselves and similar issues. We also discussed proper attire and appearance. Everyone in the class wore makeup except me. It had never been provided in my biological home; we were poor, and it wasn't a necessity.

One day, it was decided that I would be the "model" for applying makeup in class. I was a great choice, as I had none on. The teacher instructed a couple of the more "girly" girls in class to apply my makeup. There were oohs and aaaahhs throughout the class as they had their fun. When they were finished, they held up a mirror for me to admire their work. They asked me what I thought.

"I don't like it! It's too much given that I haven't worn any makeup up to this point." I exclaimed. "I feel like I'm looking at a stranger."

Several in the class agreed with me. What they had done was too much of a change in my day-to-day appearance. If they had used a lighter application, it would have been a nice improvement.

In my Personal Development class, I sat on the back row with several black women who accepted me for who I was and made me feel welcome. They were upfront with me with their questions and concerns about their lives. It was refreshing. One time we all cracked up after one of the girls told a joke.

"Alright," the teacher said. "I want the black row, I mean the back row to settle down now. You may not be disruptive to the class."

Well, no one was quite sure how to take her slip. We talked about it later and couldn't decide if she was a racist. That must really be what she thought about us and called us in her mind's eye -- "the Black Row." We began calling ourselves "the Black Row" because we agreed that we liked the sound of it. I was the only white girl on that row, but I was never made to feel out of place by any of the women with whom I sat!

I liked the structure and routine school brought to my life. I went to school Monday through Friday, did my homework at night while Mae was sleeping and Tina and Billy were working. I put in between twelve and sixteen hours a weekend at Pizza Hut. Initially, I took the bus from Falls Church into Washington every morning. One day, one of my teachers asked me to stay after class so she could talk to me when the others had gone.

"Rita, how do you get to school each day?" she asked.

"I ride the bus from Falls Church," I replied.

"I was pretty sure that was you I've seen, day after day," she replied. "I drive in with another teacher, and we pass your bus stop every morning. We've already talked about it. If you want to ride in with us in the mornings to save some money, we would be happy to pick you up. How does that sound?" she asked.

"That would be great," I said.

"Well, when we pass your bus stop, we'll stop and pick you up. If you aren't at the bus stop, we won't wait because we're required to be at school early. We can pick you up starting tomorrow if you would like."

Starting the next day, I rode in with the two teachers. It was nicer, as well as cheaper than riding the bus. I had not been looking forward to waiting out in the cold for the bus as winter approached, so I was glad my teacher had offered to give me a ride. They dropped me off after school across from the bus stop, and I only had to walk a couple of blocks to get back home.

On my walk home, I thought about the recent changes in my life: moving in with Billy and Tina, starting school to learn new skills which would open up better job opportunities for me, and finding part-time work. For the first time in a long time, I felt like I was moving forward, and I felt hopeful about what my future held for me.

Chapter 17

Forgiven & Loved

I had not had any contact with my immediate family in quite some time, so I was surprised when I received a letter from my brother, Little Ed, telling me he had gotten saved. From his brief description of what had happened, it sounded like he now had a genuine belief that Jesus was going to help him get his life turned around. I was happy for him because it sounded like he was happy.

I was hitchhiking one Sunday as I still didn't have transportation and the bus schedule was more erratic on the weekends. I had gotten picked up by a guy who seemed harmless. I was making small talk with the driver when I abruptly asked what the sign on his dashboard said. It was a white sticker. I could make neither heads nor tails of the black lines, which looked quite random to me. Just above the black lines, it said, "What Does This Say?"

He started laughing when I asked what it said, and I had no idea why he was laughing.

"You really can't see what it says?" he asked.

"I wouldn't be asking you what it says if I could see it," I responded, a bit testily.

"Okay, no need to get upset," he said. "It says 'Jesus.' Look away from it for a minute or so, and then look again to see if you can see it," he suggested.

I did as he said, and sure enough, when I looked at it again and waited a few seconds, I could see that it said "Jesus." I was perplexed that, initially, I had not been able to see it.

"That's great," he replied encouragingly. He told me his name was Gary, he worked in construction, he was a Christian, and that he loved Jesus. He asked me a few questions about myself, which I answered.

Gary told me his church had a college and career age group for people our age that met on Sunday nights, and he said the meeting usually lasted a couple of hours. He asked me if I would like to attend the meeting with him at his friends' home later that evening. I asked what they did at these meetings, and he explained that they read the Bible and talked about what they were reading and sang songs and prayed for each other. He said there were young married couples and single people who attended college or worked. He said they had refreshments at the end. He offered to pick me up around 6:15, saying he liked to get there a few minutes early. I said yes as I was curious, and it worked out since Billy and Tina were off on Sunday nights. Gary dropped me right at the house so he would know where to pick me up later. I gave him the phone number at the house in case he had to cancel for any reason.

Shortly after dinner, I was sitting on the couch, sharing a joint with Tina and Billy. I told them I had met a nice guy, and he was going to be at the house in about an hour to pick me up and take me to a Bible study. They thought I was joking because I was a bit of a prankster.

"No, I'm serious," I said, after exhaling smoke from my last hit.

Billy took the joint as I offered it to him. "Why are you doing that?" he asked.

"Why not?" I asked. "I guess I'm curious and like to check things out."

"I'll see you guys later," I said, dashing out the door at 6:15 when Gary pulled up out front. "I should be back in about three hours."

As we were driving over to the Bible study, Gary explained that the meeting was held in the home of Dan and Scotti Duis. He said Dan was an associate pastor at the nondenominational church he attended and said there were usually twenty to thirty people at the meetings, which took place downstairs in the basement because there was more room. We got there about ten minutes early, and Gary started introducing me to people. At one point, I took a cigarette out of my purse to light up, and someone asked me nicely not to smoke in the house, explaining that it was one of the house rules.

"Here we go, with all the rules," I said under my breath as I put my cigarette away.

Gary introduced me to Dan and Scotti, who were dressed in jeans and warm fall sweaters. I was expecting collars and robes as I had been exposed mostly to Catholic churches and visited an Episcopalian church once with Aunt Mary. Dan was tall with dark hair and eyes, and Scotti was short, blond, and had blue eyes. They made a handsome couple. They both welcomed me to their home, and they seemed sincere. I was a little defensive after the no-smoking incident, but these people really seemed nice. Everyone was smiling and seemed to be enjoying being together.

Dan called the meeting to order, and we all stood around in a big circle. There was silence initially, and everybody had their eyes closed. My eyes were open; I wanted to know what was going on. Then they started singing a song but not in a language I had ever heard. I figured, because it was a college group, they must be singing in the languages they were learning in college. Even though I couldn't understand it, it was very beautiful, and I really sensed a peace among these people and in the house. It was an unfamiliar but welcome sensation.

They sang a few songs in English, and a couple of people were playing guitars. Then they sang some more in the unknown language. After that, we all sat down, and someone talked about a particular passage from the Bible for about fifteen or twenty minutes and what they thought it meant and how it would apply to our lives today. I don't recollect the passage; what I do remember is that it all made sense to me, and I didn't take issue with what was said.

At the conclusion of the mini lecture, we were asked to take a few minutes before coming upstairs for refreshments to talk to the person who was sitting to the left of us and ask if they had any prayer needs. They encouraged us to pray for that person, then the person for whom we prayed would pray for us. When we were finished praying, we could come upstairs for refreshments and fellowship. The fellow to my left introduced himself as Rich and asked what he could pray for me about. I told him I was having a hard time with the ten-minute typing tests at school. I told him I had to score fifty-five words a minute with no more than three errors on two tests within five days of each other to pass the test requirements. I told him, when I was not being tested, I was timed typing about fifty-five to sixty-five words a minute. When I was being tested, my fingers just seemed to freeze, or I made too many mistakes.

Rich prayed a simple but heartfelt prayer for me, asking the Lord to help me pass my typing test requirements. Then, he asked me to pray for him about a particular relationship as he was wondering if the Lord would have him take it to the next level. I really didn't know much about prayer but just imitated what I had heard him pray for me and made it applicable to him. He seemed satisfied as he said a hearty amen at the end. He then offered to show me where the refreshments were upstairs.

There were sodas, tea, water and juices, and coffee upstairs, as well as some homemade baked goods, including some delicious oatmeal cookies. Many people walked up and introduced themselves and asked me to tell a little about myself and how I knew Gary. I told them I had met Gary today when he picked me up hitchhiking. I got a few raised eyebrows with that story, but I was also told to come again by everyone. Everyone seemed authentic and friendly, and I felt comfortable with them. All in all, I had a surprisingly nice time at the Bible study.

On the way back to the house, Gary told me that their pastor had returned from Israel and was going to be talking about the trip at a Full Gospel businessmen's meeting on Tuesday night and asked if I wanted to come. I told him Tuesday was my birthday.

He said, "Perfect. We can have dinner, and it will be my treat. How about I pick you up around 5:30 on Tuesday?"

I told him I had to be home no later than 9:00 PM so Billy and Tina could leave for work. He said that would be no problem. He would probably have me home by 8:30 PM.

Not only had he offered me a free meal, but I also had liked what I had seen that night at the Bible study. I told him I would go and thanked him for offering to treat me to dinner.

Gary picked me up on Tuesday, November 22, 1977, my twenty-second birthday, right on time. Just a few minutes later, we pulled into the Seven Corners Shopping Center in Fairfax County, Virginia. We got out of the car and headed into the S&W Cafeteria.

"You mean he's preaching in a restaurant?" I asked, completely baffled by the idea of preaching happening anywhere but inside a church. Gary explained that the Full Gospel Businessmen's Association held meetings at this restaurant on a regular basis and that there was usually a time of worship at the beginning and a guest speaker every month. He said we would have our dinner after worship was over.

The worship was led by a band that was similar to what I heard at the meeting on Sunday. Some of the people in the restaurant sang along with some of the songs. The preaching didn't really mean too much to me as it was all about Israel. I had no understanding of Israel's significance to church history, American history, or as a nation. Most of what the man spoke about was over my head. But the food was hot and warm and tasty.

Over the course of the last couple of days, I had met some people who were both authentic and content. I didn't know many folks like that and never had. There was also something else about them that I couldn't quite put my finger on. I was drawn to them. They were open and candid. This made me consider the letter from Little Ed and his salvation experience. He communicated hope and joy in his letter and some good changes in his life. When the pastor gave an altar call, I went forward to accept and acknowledge Jesus as my personal savior. A few people prayed for me, standing around me. Some of them gently laid their hands on my back or my arms while they prayed for me.

Gary was totally excited, and we sat around for a while after the "meeting" had ended, talking about getting saved and what it would mean in my life. I was totally excited as well, though, at the time, I would have been hard-pressed to explain exactly why. My life was radically altered for the better as a result of that decision, and I knew it would result in even more changes in how I lived my life. I had no idea what that would look like. An immediate result was that I felt peace deep within my being. I had not experienced that sense of peace since I had cried out in prayer to God as a ten-year-old. And at that time, it had been very short-lived.

I knew I still had a lot of problems to overcome and the consequences of bad choices with which to live. I also knew I would find a way, and things would eventually work out. Practically speaking, I had already made some changes to try to get my life headed in a better direction. The practical changes I had made hadn't stirred up this exciting anticipation I now felt reverberating within me. With my surrender to Jesus, I actually felt a new hope about my future that I hadn't had before. I had held onto hope as a child for years, but the day my mother turned on me after we had talked about the sexual abuse, I had lost all hope for anything better or different than what I had always known. "At spes non fracta" is Latin, and it means "but hope is not crushed or broken." My hope had been crushed repeatedly as an abused child and adolescent. But now, I was feeling practically intoxicated by the hope that now surged within me.

I was born again on my twenty-second birthday -- in a restaurant, of all places. On that day, I let go of a whole lot of preconceived notions I had clung to about God. I let go of some of the anger and hate I had held in my heart towards the Lord because He had not answered my prayers as I thought He should have when I was ten, and again at fifteen when I ran away to the streets of Washington, D.C. Some heavy weights were lifted from me that day as I scratched the surface of what it meant to be freed from a life of sin.

Gary invited me to church on Sunday morning. He said the church met in a high school in Vienna, and he would pick me up around 9:30. He said they sang songs, looked at scripture passages, and prayed for people, much like the meeting I had already attended. He said church involved many more people of all ages, and the time of worship and the time in the Word were a bit longer than in the college career group setting.

On Sunday morning, I was sitting in the high school auditorium, listening to the same man I had heard speak at the restaurant. He was talking about someone who might be embarrassed about speaking in tongues publicly. I had no idea what he was talking about. He asked if there was anyone in the group who had never publicly spoken in tongues. I raised my hand. Gary almost intervened, but then he just chuckled to himself and let me be. Sure enough, the pastor beckoned me to come up in front of all those people. I could tell, by what he was saying as he continued to talk to the congregation, that he had been referring to someone who already "spoke in tongues," but they didn't do so publicly because they were embarrassed or self-conscious or maybe lacked understanding.

"Excuse me, sir," I interrupted him. "I have never heard of speaking in tongues. I have no idea what you are talking about."

He chuckled, just like Gary, and asked that his elders come forward and pray for me so I would receive the gift of speaking in tongues. Fortunately, no one tried to explain it to me, which I believe was wise on their part. The elders laid their hands on me like those people had on Tuesday night, and they asked the Lord to baptize me in His Holy Spirit with the manifestation of speaking in tongues. Though I lacked any understanding at that point, there was no resistance in me because I was around genuine, honest, contented people. I didn't feel vulnerable at all. For the first time in my life, I felt like I was truly in a safe place, and, as a result, I was pretty open to new ideas.

As I stood there, I began to utter new words that I had never heard before and lifted my hands in surrender as did others throughout the congregation. Peace flooded me from the top of my head to the tip of my toes. I was fully immersed in the very tangible presence of God. Closing my eyes, I lost all awareness of anything or anyone around me as I basked and delighted in the realness and warmth of God's presence. After a few minutes of stillness in His presence, I returned to my seat.

Gary couldn't believe that I was speaking in tongues and filled with the Holy Spirit on my first Sunday back in a church after years of absence. He elaborated further on the drive back home that when I had given my heart to the Lord the past Tuesday night, I had been filled with the Holy Spirit and that praying in tongues was just a manifestation of being filled with the Holy Spirit. He was telling me that, just like a baby starts out with a limited vocabulary, I would initially have a limited vocabulary with tongues. He said as I practiced speaking and singing in tongues on a regular basis, my vocabulary would increase.

As I set apart quiet times to read my Bible, pray, and sing songs to God, I used this new gift of tongues. When I was either singing or praying in tongues, I felt a real connection to God. I didn't understand what I was praying or singing, but knowing that I was praying with my spirit, which had been born again, I was okay. The scripture says to pray for understanding when one speaks in an unknown tongue, so I did pray for understanding as well. Often after singing in tongues, I would sing genuine words in English of praise and adoration to Jesus which I took to be the interpretation of tongues.

My new routine in life on Sundays was going to church with Gary in the morning and going to the college career-age meeting in the evening. He said it was no problem for him to pick me up and to get me home. During this season, I was meeting new people and learning about God and what it meant to be a Christian and to walk by the spirit. I loved the times of worship at the beginning of these meetings, where everyone just sang before the Lord. They had the words up on a screen, using an overhead projector, so even if I didn't know the songs, I could sing along and eventually learn them. The speakers in both venues talked about God and His character and discussed passages from the Bible. I was encouraged listening to them, and my hope was growing. I found myself surrendering myself to the Lord over and over because so much of what I heard really moved my heart.

Before I was saved and started going to church, I smoked pot just about every day. I smoked a joint or two after finishing my homework long after Mae had been put to bed. I smoked on the weekends after work. Pot was very much a part of my daily life, so I continued to smoke a joint or share a pipe with the folks at home before heading for the Sunday evening meeting.

Gary picked me up, as usual, one evening for the gathering in Vienna. I guess he smelled the pot on me because he began to tell me that, as a believer, I really should not be smoking pot. I told him God had created the plant and wanted us to partake of its many benefits. He told me that God would not want any of His children breaking the law by smoking pot. He told me the Devil was just as real as God, and the Devil would be thrilled that a believer was smoking pot because the pot would dull spiritual sensitivity. Being dull would make a believer less useful to God.

I don't remember exactly how I responded, but Gary, walking in a measure of spiritual maturity, dropped it because he could tell I wasn't in a place to hear him on the subject. It was very wise on his part. I can't say how I would've responded if he had really pushed the issue, but I could have lost all interest in continuing to pursue anything having to do with God.

Gary didn't bring up pot again, but I had learned that he prayed about everything. He trusted the Holy Spirit to lead me into all truth, including the truth about pot.

As the Christmas season approached, some of the girls from school and I had talked about smuggling in some beer for the party we were going to have at school before the holiday break. I had just gotten a case of Heineken for my birthday from Billy and Tina. I wasn't much of a beer drinker, so this would be a good way of getting rid of it. Unfortunately, I didn't understand that carbonated beverages shouldn't travel in a thermos. I never gave it a second thought as I poured the beer into the thermos.

I climbed into the car that morning, as usual, when my teachers stopped to get me near the bus stop. Seeing that I was carrying more than normal because of the party, one of the teachers offered to take one of my bags. I gave her the bag with the thermos full of beer. Shortly thereafter, the teacher wanted to know what was in the bag as the contents were leaking all over her skirt.

"Rita, this smells like beer," she exclaimed. "Why would you be bringing beer to school?"

When we got into the school building, she told me to come into the restroom with her. She tried to use hand soap and paper towels to clean herself up. She lectured me on bringing alcohol into school and warned me about how much trouble I could face. She made me dump the rest of the beer into the sink. She told me not to discuss the incident with my classmates at all and to give no explanation for why I didn't have the beer as promised. She was gracious, considering that she taught her classes throughout the day smelling like a brewery, and would certainly have to answer to someone in school administration for that. There was no doubt I would certainly be in trouble and possibly even be expelled from school.

I don't know what my teacher said to those in charge, but none of the feared consequences were forthcoming. I was very grateful to her.

A couple of weeks later, on a Sunday afternoon, Mae was napping. Tina, Billy, and Lee, Billy's brother, were in the living room taking some hits from a joint. I was sitting on the couch talking with them. The joint came to me, and I paused with it in my hand for a moment, then passed it on without smoking any of it. Everyone in the room was staring at me with their mouths hanging open. I was behaving totally out of character. I had never said no to pot.

"Listen, guys, I really feel great already," I tried to explain. "I have a peace inside me I never had before. I just don't need this right now. No judgment intended, but I don't want it."

I started saying no to pot on a regular basis at that point. No one was pressuring me to smoke it either; they seemed to respect the changes I was making. I prayed and asked God to help me continue to say no to drugs because I longed to walk by the spirit and not in my old ways.

However, there was also cocaine in the house occasionally, and they always shared it with me. I couldn't currently afford it, so I had always gratefully accepted up to this point. Knowing my own weaknesses, I was pretty sure I wouldn't be able to say no to cocaine if it were offered. I was learning to discern His will and His purposes in my day-to-day life. I felt like the Lord was teaching me that I could do all things through Him, right out of the scripture.

I had been in my room, one Sunday afternoon, with the door shut, finishing up some homework that was due the next day. When I came into the kitchen to get a drink, Billy and his brother, Lee, were sitting at the table, passing a razor blade through some cocaine on a cutting board to make sure it was fine and easy to snort. Sure enough, they offered me some. And then something happened that I absolutely never expected. I thanked them but said I didn't want any and kept heading for the refrigerator to get a cold drink. God's grace has risen up in me in almost a tangible way, and saying no was not the overwhelming struggle I had feared. The words that came to my mind were, I have real peace now. Cocaine cannot add to what I already have.

I had made an appointment to see the pastor of the church to talk about my current situation and to see about clarification for direction in moving forward with my life. As we talked together, I gave Pastor Derrel a brief recounting of my life and told him I really wanted to grow and learn more about the Lord. Pastor Derrel told me there was a couple who attended the church, who were named Carleton and Katharine Raiford, and they had opened their home, the "Farm," to those who had painful backgrounds like mine and helped them grow in the Lord. He said Carleton was one of the elders at our church and asked me if I was interested in exploring that option further. When I said yes, he gave me their telephone number and told me he would let them know I would be calling.

Pastor Derrel said he was amazed at all the good things the Lord had done in my life already, and he was looking forward to seeing what else would happen. He expressed genuine sympathy for the many pains I had had to endure. He asked me if I knew how important it was to forgive those who had hurt me, and he shared some scriptures with me. He also recommended I attend a seminar that could be helpful to me as a new believer. He prayed with me and asked God to heal the wounds of my heart and to lead me into what He had next for me. At the end of our meeting, he told me not to hesitate to contact him if I needed anything else. He was very kind, and he seemed authentic. I was comfortable with him, and I liked him.

I talked with Gary about the seminar Pastor Derrel had recommended and asked him if he knew anything about it. He said it was really beneficial for spiritual growth, and he had been before. He said he would let me know when the next one was scheduled after he made some inquiries. He said he would plan to attend as well.

At the next Sunday evening meeting, I was talking with Gary and a small group of people about the pastor's recommendation that I consider moving to the Farm. Ruth, one of my new friends in the group, told me she thought that would be good for me as a new believer. She said she had lived there, and Kitty and Carleton had really helped her immensely. Ruth suggested I set up a time to meet with them and offered to drive me to the Farm in Manassas, about 45 minutes from the church in Vienna. She insisted on taking me and said she would enjoy some time on the Farm again while I was talking with Kitty and Carleton.

Chapter 18

The Farm

The following weekend, Ruth and I enjoyed talking on the drive out to Manassas. She shared some of her testimony with me and had nothing but good things to say about the Raifords. She said she was hoping she wasn't making living on the Farm sound easy, though, because there would be nothing easy about it. The Farm had been nicknamed "Sandpaper University" by Ruth and several others who had lived there because God used the time to sand off a person's rough spots, which could be quite a painful process. She insisted if one wanted to look like Jesus, the sandpaper process was a necessity. I appreciated hearing about her experiences at the Farm, which made me feel like I had more of a realistic idea of what it would be like to live there.

When we arrived, Carleton and Katharine warmly welcomed us into their home, giving us some refreshments. Katharine told me she went by Kitty. Ruth, book in hand, excused herself to find a quiet nook to read in until we were done.

"So, Pastor Derrel sent you?" Kitty asked, offering me a seat in the living room.

I confirmed that he had. She and Carleton asked me what I was doing with my life currently. I told them about school being my biggest priority, so I could get a job and get back on my feet financially. I told them about my arrangements with Billy and Tina and that I was working part-time at Pizza

Hut to bring in a little money. I also told them I loved the family with whom I lived but felt it was time to make a move.

They inquired why I didn't move back home with my family while I was in school. I informed them that when I was fifteen, I had run away from my abusive home and had never been back. I added that my family wanted nothing to do with me since then, so staying with them was not an option for me. Kitty said they would like to talk about that later if I was open and then asked what I was doing for transportation. I told them about the DWI and losing my license, but also that I could get it reinstated at this point and buy a car but just didn't have the money to do so while attending school full time. I also told them my insurance was going to be very expensive because of the DWI ticket.

One of the stipulations for people moving in, according to Carleton, was that they have their own transportation as that was not something they could commit to providing. They said the bus didn't make it out to their area, so that would not be an option. Carleton prayed that the Lord would give us wisdom in how He would have us move forward. He assured me they would be in touch once they had time to pray about it.

A few days later, after I had gotten Mae tucked in for the night and I was getting started on my shorthand homework, the telephone rang. It was Kitty Raiford. She told me she and Carleton had prayed about it and would like to extend an invitation for me to move in at the Farm. She said even though I didn't have a car, Carleton worked in Washington, D.C., just a few blocks from the school I was attending. Although it wasn't the normal arrangement, they had with people living there and they felt like it would work for me to ride with him in the mornings. But the drive took an hour and a half one way, and I would have to be ready to leave when he was ready, as I couldn't make him late. Also, since I was finished with school before he was finished with work, I would have to fill my time until I could meet him in the parking garage where he left his car during the day.

Kitty asked me what I thought about the proposed arrangements, and I told her it sounded great. I said I wanted to give Billy and Tina at least two weeks' notice so they could find someone to be at their house overnight for Mae. I would also need to give two weeks' notice at Pizza Hut. We agreed that if I could work out the details, I would move to the Farm in two weeks, over the weekend. I was very excited, as I felt like moving to the Farm was a direct answer to prayer.

Saying good-bye to Mae was pretty tough; we had grown quite close. I didn't have a car to drive when I wanted to go back to visit, so I didn't make her any promises about when I would see her next. I did tell her I was going to miss her very much.

At the end of December 1977, I moved to the Farm. Gary helped me load up my belongings and drove me to Manassas. Upon arrival, I was taken to my bedroom at the top of the stairs. The room had a big window that looked out over the driveway and the front of the house. A nightstand stood between the twin beds, and there was a dresser along one wall. The room also had a good-sized closet. A couple of paintings hung on the walls. On my level, there were two more bedrooms, a large sitting room, and a large bathroom. Currently, I was the only person staying upstairs, so it would be part of my responsibility to keep that bathroom clean and ready for company at all times. Apparently, it was not unusual for people to come to stay with them for a few days.

A little later, Kitty showed me where things were in the pantry and told me to make myself at home. She said to make a list of what I would need from the grocery store, so I would have food for breakfast and lunch. I told her I would be willing to cook on the weekends, and she said just give her a list of ingredients I would need for the meals I wanted to cook. She showed me the calendar in the kitchen, which listed nights they wouldn't be home for dinner, so I would need to plan and cook my own dinner those nights.

She then asked me if I smoked, and I said yes. She said there could be no smoking on the property; Kitty said they just didn't want the smell or the fire risk in the house. The Farm was situated in a very remote spot, and there were no fire hydrants nearby. She pointed out my bedroom window way up the gravelly driveway to where we turned in from the main road. She said I could smoke there and keep a soda can in the bushes for the butts, so I wouldn't leave a mess. That was not going to be fun or easy, but it was the rule. She also said there could be no alcohol or drugs on the property, and I shouldn't be doing things like that anymore since I had given myself to the Lord. She reminded me I was not my own anymore and that I had been bought with a price. She was not patronizing or condescending when she said these things, just very matter of fact.

I had arrived early in the afternoon and gotten my things unloaded fairly quickly. After a couple of hours, I had unpacked the items for the bathroom, filled the dresser drawers and the closet, and selected which bed I would sleep in.

Kitty asked me if I had had additional belongings I would need to store. I told her I actually had about fifteen or twenty boxes stored in a friend's basement. She told me I was more than welcome to move all my things to the Farm and store boxes upstairs in the barn on the property because I was probably going to live at the Farm for a while.

She also told me we were having company at dinner that night. Roger and Amy Green would be joining us. They, too, attended Christian Assembly and the Tuesday evening meetings at the Farm. I offered her my assistance in dinner preparations, and she asked if I would set the table, which helped me figure out where dishes and glasses and flatware were kept.

Other than the brief exposure I had at secretarial school; I hadn't received any instruction about manners. We had chicken as part of the meal that night, and I couldn't tell from looking at it whether I needed to use a knife and fork or if I could just pick it up to eat it. I decided to eat my salad until I saw someone else at the table eat the chicken, and whatever they did, I would do. Well, eventually, one of the guests picked up the chicken and started to eat it, so I did the same. Kitty corrected me and told me that as the chicken was covered in a sauce, it should be eaten with a knife and fork. I was embarrassed and made the situation worse by pointing out that a guest had picked up the chicken, so I thought it was okay. It was awkward for a couple of minutes, but Roger made a joke and helped us all move on.

After dinner, I helped clear the table and load the dishwasher and offered to do the hand washables. Kitty accepted my offer, and I started washing the dishes while they moved to the living room. I had to pass through the living room where they were visiting, so I told them I was going to go upstairs and get my homework done. I let Amy and Roger know I enjoyed meeting them and apologized if I embarrassed them earlier during dinner. They said to forget about it, everything was fine.

I hadn't been upstairs even ten minutes when a soft knocking came on my door.

"Rita, it's Kitty. Can I come in for a minute?" she asked.

"Sure," I responded.

She opened the door and came in and sat on the edge of the bed where I was sitting with my shorthand book.

"Rita, I have a feeling I embarrassed you at dinner tonight, and I am so sorry. That was not my intention. Could you forgive me for being insensitive over something so silly?" she asked.

I was completely astounded. She hadn't beaten me, stabbed me, thrown hot coffee on me, or even called me terrible names. She had only embarrassed me, and here she was, my first night in her home, telling me she was sorry for something she had said and asking for my forgiveness! She didn't even justify herself by saying it was really my fault, if only I knew the proper way to eat chicken, and so on.

Assuring her, I forgave her and admitted to being a bit embarrassed. I explained I hadn't known what I was supposed to do and hadn't been taught manners growing up. She told me she could teach me some etiquette when we didn't have company coming over for dinner. I told her I would like that. Then she hugged me and told me she had to get back to her company.

I hadn't spent much time around people like Kitty, sincere, real, and sensitive. This kind of behavior was new to me, and I really liked it! My mother had done far worse things to me and had only apologized once, yet still blamed me for what she had done to me.

Once I moved out to the Farm, I usually rode to church on Sunday mornings with Carleton and Kitty. If they had plans after church, it wasn't too difficult to find someone else from the Manassas fellowship group to drop me off at home. Sometimes, I would stay in town with Gary or someone else from the Sunday night fellowship group. Once the evening meeting was over, Gary drove me back to Manassas. He was a good friend who made a lot of sacrifices for me.

After a couple of weeks of living on the Farm, life fell into a routine that revolved around commuting, schooling, dinner time, and homework. Carleton and I had some very interesting talks on the way into the city and on the way out. He would ask me what I wanted to discuss, and, if I didn't have a topic, he most surely did. We often listened to Dr. Vernon McGee on the drive-in. I liked Dr. McGee; he discussed concepts of the Christian faith in a simple and straightforward manner, and he talked about issues I felt were relevant to me as a new believer. Carleton and I would discuss the message when the program ended.

One day after school, when I was walking the few blocks to Carleton's parking garage, there was a person walking towards me who looked somewhat familiar. As they got closer, both of us were staring at one another with our mouths hanging open and came to a complete stop on the sidewalk. It was my older sister Darlene, whom I had seen only at family weddings or funerals since running away from home in 1969, eight years ago.

"Oh, my God! I can't believe it's you," I exclaimed. "What are you doing here?"

She told me she had been in training meetings in Washington over the last several days for her job. She asked me what I was doing in the city. I told her I was attending a secretarial school a few blocks away and was meeting my ride home. I scribbled my phone number on a piece of paper and told her it was the number where I was staying.

Darlene said she was still living at home, so I might not hear from her right away. She explained that she would be getting her own place within the month, and once she had moved out and settled in her new place, she would definitely call me. I told her I had missed her and the rest of the siblings terribly, but I had done what was necessary. I gave her a hug, which made her a little uncomfortable, as ours had not been a touchy-feely family. I told her I really looked forward to hearing from her once she got moved and understood completely that it would be impossible until then.

I couldn't believe I ran into Darlene just walking down the street in Washington. I told Carleton about running into her when we were settled into the car. He thought it was rather amazing as well.

Meanwhile, it weighed on me that I was unable to obtain work while living at the Farm because I didn't have a car. The Farm was about ten minutes from town. The country roads were not designed for pedestrian traffic, so walking into town was not really an option. Besides, even if I walked in after school, by the time I put in three or four hours, it would be too dark to walk home on those roads. All I had was the $68 a month that came as part of my student loan monies. I wasn't charged anything for room and board because Kitty and Carleton knew I didn't have much money. So, I made myself available to Kitty on Saturdays for help with cleaning to try to feel I was at least contributing something. With Billy and Tina, I had known I was providing them a needed service watching Mae while they worked. At the Farm, it was a little tougher. I often offered to help with housework, and I washed a lot of dishes after dinner. Kitty told me not to worry about the finances; she said they had prayed about having me live there, and they knew I was without a car or much of an income when they agreed to me moving in with them. She said when I finished school and was finally working, we would discuss my "rent."

All the people who lived in Manassas and made the long drive to Vienna for church on Sundays met at the Farm in the barn on Tuesday nights at 7:00 PM for what was referred to as Home Group meetings. They were all married, and most of them had kids. The meeting lasted for about an hour and a half and included some worship time. During worship, one of the women might share a testimony about how the Lord had ministered to their family that week. One of the men might ask for prayer and be pretty specific about the need. Then one of the men from the group would teach about what he saw in his personal study of the Bible. It was understandable and applicable to my life. I was very encouraged and sensed God's presence with us throughout our time together. Afterward, we would go into the house for refreshments. Most everyone brought something to share, so there were plenty of treats. There were a lot of families from Christian Assembly that lived in Manassas, and they seemed to be particularly comfortable and open with one another. Most of them had known Kitty and Carleton for quite some time.

Besides getting together on Tuesday evenings, the Raifords often had a family from the group come for dinner during the week or on the weekend. This was a very social group. It was easier to get to know them when they came for dinner than in the Tuesday night setting. But even on Tuesday nights, someone would often share a prayer request, letting the rest of the group know something, in particular, they were having a hard time with or why they might need wisdom on how to move forward or even share the need for healing in their bodies.

The Raifords also had a bookshelf out in the barn, and people brought canned goods and peanut butter and pasta and paper goods and other things like that and left them on the shelf. There were plastic bags on the bottom shelf, and if anyone needed anything, they were to take it, and no explanations were necessary.

I was brand-new in the Lord when I moved there, and I carried a lot of baggage with me. There were lots of rough spots that had not yet come in contact with God's sandpaper. In spite of that, I felt welcome because the Raifords had welcomed me. Many of the women spoke to me after my first

Tuesday night meeting, and several very meaningful relationships would develop over the next several months.

In January of 1978, I attended a class at church on physical baptism by total immersion. Then, I was signed up along with several others to be baptized. We used another congregation's baptismal, as we were still meeting in the high school on Sunday mornings. It was an awesome time. Many from church, including Gary, attended to support us in our decision to obey the scripture's instruction to be baptized. Carleton joined Pastor Derrel in the baptismal when it was my turn, as he was assuming a lot of responsibility for me by having me live in his home, and he was one of the elders at church.

Sometime in early spring, I had started calling Carleton and Kitty "Pa" and "Ma" instead of their given names. It just happened. These two people loved me, encouraged me, affirmed me, and challenged me in ways I hadn't known prior to moving in with them. They had gradually learned more about my history with my extremely dysfunctional and abusive parents. They encouraged me to forgive them so that I could truly move on with my life. Many others who had lived with the Raifords called them similar names. They had opened their home to many young, broken people and helped them move from the past into the present.

Life at the Farm was a wonderful experience for me. I was living with people who had been married for many years, and their love for one another was obvious. They had their little disagreements, but they quickly resolved their issues with love and forgiveness. They didn't scream and yell at one another and destroy one another's possessions. Seeing their relationship, compared to what I had seen between my parents, gave me hope. Pa and Ma lived an open and transparent life before me. They were always available to me. They taught me a lot by the way they lived their lives and their interaction with others. What I loved the most was that they were real. They didn't present themselves one way to outsiders, then live a completely different life behind closed doors.

Ma Raiford did have a hard time believing my real mother didn't love me. I told her if my mother did love me, I could not recall one demonstration of that love. The many abuses in many forms that I had suffered directly from her didn't ever appear to be expressions of love. I had sent letters over the years and birthday cards and never had any response (my grandmother had provided Cathy's address once I was finished with high school). I attempted reconciliation, but she had never responded. What was I to do with that?

Ma had two daughters of her own, and she loved them dearly from their infancy. She just couldn't comprehend being given the gift of a child and not loving that child; it made no sense to her.

I was pretty sure I had been perceived as a burden by my parents and not a gift. On top of that, I was also fairly certain my mother had some type of mental illness. A normal person couldn't do those things to a child and live with themselves as though all was fine with the world. My mother couldn't accept reality; I was her child, and her denial didn't change the situation. I have no idea what reality she had created for herself that maybe insulated her from all the pain associated with me as her daughter.

Though my own immediate family had forsaken me, I met and was accepted into a new family among this gathering of believers. I met a lot of loving, sincere, and genuine people here when I was still carrying quite the attitude. I had been accepted as I was, broken and angry. They all had their own relationships with Jesus, and they knew I was a work in progress. I was far from the finished product.

My mother's side of the family had been very good to me and hadn't forsaken me. They gave me a home when Social Services had run out of options and when their own home was already full of people. They had been willing to give me a home long before I moved in with them, but my mother wouldn't hear of it. If it hadn't been for my mother's parents, I probably would have never finished high school. I always longed for relationships to be healed with my immediate, biological family. But it was not something I had been able to make happen. Until my brother contacted me by mail and I ran into Darlene in Washington, a connection on any level hadn't been possible.

As May was approaching and I was finishing school, I started praying about where I was going to work and how all of that was going to come together. God provided for me in amazing ways. One of the women from the group, Denise, approached me and said she thought we were about the same size and that I was probably going to need a more professional wardrobe when I started interviewing for jobs and actually started working. She invited me to come over on Saturday at around eleven, so I could try some clothes on and see if I could build up my wardrobe until I was on my feet. She said when I was on my feet financially and could buy clothes for work, I could return her things. Denise stressed there was no hurry as she had recently quit her job to be home with her first child. Ma offered to drop me off. She would be doing errands on that end of town and would pick me up in a couple of hours. Denise's clothes fit me nicely and added greatly to what I had to choose from for clothing. Plus, the clothing was professional, which I would need, according to the personal development teacher at school.

My next challenge was how I would get back and forth to work. The local insurance agent I had contacted informed me that before I could go to the DMV and apply to have my license reinstated, I would have to show proof of insurance. He was willing to sell me a policy, but it would be a bit pricey because of the serious charges that led to me losing my license in the first place. Ma told me she had been given some money anonymously by someone who met with us on Tuesdays, so I could purchase the insurance I needed. She gave me a ride to the bank, and I purchased a cashier's check with the cash to mail to the insurance agent.

I had to pass a driving test with the department of motor vehicles again since I had lost my license. The lady who took me out for the road test told me if it was up to her, I would never get my license back. I guess she had seen my record, which reflected a great disregard for the law, as I had multiple tickets culminating with driving while intoxicated. Now, I had to drive while she would be looking for anything and everything I might do wrong. I sent a quick prayer up to the Lord asking for His help because if she didn't pass me, I was going to have a lot of new problems. On top of all that, the woman didn't put her seat belt on. I didn't know if it was deliberate on her part, but I figured she was probably testing me.

"I am sorry, ma'am," I said, "but I do need you to put your seat belt on before I can start driving. Please."

She huffed and puffed, but she put her seat belt on. I think it was a trap, but I didn't get caught. I sensed she was frustrated because she wanted me to get caught, and then she could deny me a license. Somehow, I passed my test with the scariest, meanest testing agent ever.

At the end of my test, I told her I was very sorry for what I had done and was very grateful no one had gotten hurt because of my recklessness. I told her I didn't drink anymore, so this wouldn't be something that would happen again with me. I also told her that I realized how much of a privilege it was to be able to drive, and I had really missed the freedom to get myself to the places I needed to be, and I wouldn't take it for granted. If she softened at all, she didn't show it as she sent me to the person who would take my picture for my license.

I thanked the Lord profusely for letting me pass somehow, even with all that extra stress because of the unbending woman who administered the road test. Now, I just needed a car, and with no income, that was the next big challenge. I prayed about it and told the Lord I was sorry I had made such a mess of my life, but I really needed His help in resolving this transportation issue.

Someone told me about a Ford Galaxy for sale for $500 and said it would probably meet my needs initially. Pa went with me to look the car over, and he reported no problems with it. I asked God to make a way for me if that was the car He had for me. The church ended up giving me a check to buy the car. I was amazed and overwhelmed by how a new wardrobe, the money for insurance, and a car had fallen into place for me! What freedom I had with a new set of wheels! Once I had my car, I didn't mind the drive to Vienna for church and continued to attend the Sunday evening fellowship. I was building relationships with several of these people and wanted to continue doing so.

I finished the training at the secretarial school in May and was hired by a temp agency while sending my resume out, seeking a more permanent position.

In early June, I attended an unsaved friend's graduation party. Inevitably, there was some pot there, and I ended up smoking some of it without giving much thought to what I was doing. As the others became a bit high from smoking the pot and began laughing over stupid things that weren't really funny, I let the joint pass without participating further. But the damage was done. I was mad at myself for blowing my opportunity to tell these people about the Lord. Additionally, because I hadn't smoked any in so long, I couldn't figure out what I had thought was so great about pot and why I had smoked so much of it and so often. Now it seemed like a waste of money and time.

I went back to the Farm that evening and told Pa I needed to talk to him. I told him he had to promise he wouldn't tell Ma Raiford what I was getting ready to tell him. This was my first serious infraction since moving in, and I had no idea how he was going to respond. After I had confessed, he said he wouldn't tell her. I told him how sorry I was and how stupid I felt.

"Are you planning to ever smoke it again?" he asked.

"No way," I exclaimed.

"That's good to hear," he said. Then he hollered for Ma to come into the room for a minute.

"You said you weren't going to tell her!" I exclaimed.

"I'm not telling her. You are," he said with a determined expression on his face. So I repeated my tale of woe to her. Ma asked me if I planned to continue smoking pot, and I said no. They told me they forgave me and prayed for me and thanked the Lord for working in my life. I never smoked pot again.

In late July, I was hired as a full-time secretary by Fairfax City Hall and worked for the Department of Parks and Recreation and the Department of Public Information. I answered the phone, took payments and registrations for Parks and Recreation programs, answered questions about the city's bus schedule and routes and rates, and typed up Public Information memos that went into the newspaper.

I shared an office with the secretary for the City Manager. When she was out for the day, I did whatever work he generated as well.

I had a full-time job with paid vacation, medical benefits, and I loved working from 8:00 AM to 5:00 PM, Monday through Friday. It was great to have my evenings and weekends free for other plans.

The Fairfax City police department was located on the first floor. Shortly after starting the new job, I was called to the first floor to talk to the Chief of Police about my arrest for Public Intoxication, Assaulting a Police Officer, and the DWI that came up during my background check. I answered his questions honestly. I told him about getting saved and not living that type of life anymore. At the end of our discussion, he said he was satisfied with my answers and didn't think it was necessary to take any further action. He congratulated me on my new job and said he hoped I liked it.

Chapter 19

Bob

One of the new people I met and hit it off with was a young mother of four, Andrea, a fellow believer, married to a man who didn't share her beliefs but didn't prevent her from attending church. She invited me to visit her at her home one evening. While I was there, I met a guy named Bob, who wasn't saved. He rented a room in their basement. He ended up joining Andrea and me for a game of Scrabble. Her kids were down for the night, and her husband was out. Bob easily won the game, but he was a terrible winner and he was arrogant. After he thanked us for the game, he retired to his room downstairs.

Andrea confided in me that she had been trying to get him to visit the church. She sensed he might be open to exploring new ideas. She asked me to pray that he would come one Sunday morning. Andrea was quite the evangelist at heart. She was sure when he encountered the genuine presence of God; Bob would get his life turned around too. I told her I would certainly be praying for him, and we prayed for him before I left that evening.

The next Sunday morning, I was sitting with my friend Fran at church when I saw Bob walk in and take a seat. I whispered to Fran and asked her to take notes for me because I would be praying for Bob throughout the service. I told her I had met him at Andrea's, and she had been trying to convince him to visit her church for a long time. I pointed him out to her. Then I bowed my head that November 5, 1978 and prayed for Bob throughout the sermon.

A member of the congregation, Dave, came forward, whispered something into Pastor Derrel's ear, and went up on stage and sat down at the piano. Partway through the song, we heard Bob sobbing. Jesus met him right where he was and gloriously changed his life that day! Andrea and I were so excited.

When Bob and Andrea returned home after church, Willy was sitting in the living room watching a show and smoking pot. "Oh, no! Not you too!" he exclaimed after taking one look at Bob. Willy knew that Bob had been saved without anyone having said anything! He saw a new creation! Bob didn't look like the same person Willy had seen walk out the door for church that morning.

"Afraid so," Bob responded, grinning from ear to ear.

"All of Willy's pot-smoking buddies are getting saved," Andrea said with a smile. "He's finding it harder and harder to find someone who wants to get high."

Bob was saved almost one year after I was. His experience caused me to look back and see how much my life had changed in just under a year because of my relationship with God. I was humbled and grateful. I was also amazed at how different I was and how much better my life was. So much had changed in such a short period of time! For example, once I was saved, I believed sex outside of marriage was no longer an option for me. I hadn't discussed sex with anyone, but my views and behavior had completely changed! Though I once had lived waiting for my next high, I had quit doing drugs. My choice of words had been so terrible I could probably have made a sailor blush with my frequent outbursts. Not so anymore. I had also quit smoking cigarettes, which was the most difficult undertaking. I had been smoking regularly, starting around age thirteen, and had gotten up to a minimum of three packs a day over the last few years. The first three weeks of quitting had been very rough, and I wasn't sure I could do it. I had cried out to the Lord for help and flushed my body with lots of water and fresh fruit to try to get rid of the toxins faster. It took most of that year to get over the desire, but I was finally free from my nicotine addiction. I don't know how else to say it, but I was a "softer" and nicer person. I had been so hard before meeting the Lord.

I was still spending quite a bit of time with Gary, and he would often sit with Fran and me at church. Occasionally, we went out to eat after church, and I was finally paying my own way. Gary was a good friend. At times I was frustrated in the relationship because I wondered if he wanted something more. I wasn't going to second guess him. I believed if he wanted something more, he was going to have to tell me!

Meanwhile, I told Bob about our Tuesday night meetings at the Farm and invited him to join us since he lived in Manassas. He started coming. He also asked me if I wanted to ride together to various functions at the church, which was forty-five minutes away. There might be a class, or teaching spread out over four weeks in the evenings, or a worship or prayer service. Bob said it seemed dumb for both of us to drive. We also started riding to Sunday morning service together. Bob and I did a lot of talking on our forty-five-minute drive to church and on the forty-five-minute drive back. I was grateful to spend so much extra time with someone who had recently accepted Christ, and it was nice to have another newbie with whom to discover all that we had been given and all that we had been freed from with our decision to embrace Christ.

Bob would often come in the house upon arriving at the Farm and spend some time talking with Ma and Pa when they were around. One of the things he talked to them about his current living situation. He was finding it challenging to live someplace, where he had easy access to pot all the time.

Shortly after his conversation with the Raifords, Bob moved in with a young married couple, Brent and Diane, who were Christians. Brent was a musician who played guitar and sang. They went to a church in Sterling, and they shared Bob's interest in the Lord and music. Bob had been the lead guitarist and a vocalist in a band before getting saved. He honored his contract with them and then moved on to playing music with Brent and his band.

Our Tuesday night fellowship was a wonderful group of people in healthy relationships. Pa and Ma being the leaders, contributed to the overall health of the group. There was not a clique. These were people in genuine, loving relationships with one another. It was an amazing community! I really felt like we had something unique, and Bob and I both benefitted deeply by beginning our walk with the Lord surrounded by these people.

Several of the men from the Tuesday night fellowship spent time with Bob and greatly encouraged him in his growth in the Lord. They introduced him to the concordance and some other books they thought were great tools for understanding the Bible and studying it. He was reading the Bible all the time and was always full of questions. The men answered some of his questions for him but also helped him find the tools to find the answers for himself.

Acting the part of matchmaker, several of the Tuesday night ladies were making suggestions to me about Bob. Since there were no other single guys coming on Tuesdays, Bob would have to do in their minds. I told them it wasn't going to happen. I assured them that we were spending time together for practical reasons.

Bob and I developed a wonderful friendship because we were not interested in one another. We weren't trying to impress one another. We were able to be ourselves with each other, and it was refreshing. He had grown up with no sisters and enjoyed learning about women from a different perspective--not that I was a typical female. I very rarely used makeup and wasn't caught up in the latest fashions. My femininity had not been encouraged and living in three different homes during high school had not helped the situation. Ma Raiford was a wonderful influence on me about what a real woman was, and she showed me the world's definition was definitely skewed. She also taught me that if I gave myself to knowing God, I would know myself and what I was to do with my life because He had created me and knew me better than anyone. She said the Lord had a purpose for me even as I was developing in my mother's womb! Ma helped me look at things through a brand-new lens!

The cold winter months had passed, and the days finally offered warmer weather. Flowers and plants were starting to bloom, and there was a fresh smell in the air. With all the new life bursting forth around me, I found my heart was in a different place when it came to Bob. I was beginning to appreciate him as a person. He spent a lot of time reading the Bible and had already written a couple of songs for the Lord. He had a way of taking complicated concepts and presenting them in a way that made them easier to understand. He was handsome and smart. I wondered if he was thinking about me in a different light too. As I was starting to care more for Bob, I was afraid my love for a man would cause me to lose my focus on the Lord as my number one priority. I didn't voice this fear to anyone. Instead, I cried out to God about it privately in prayer.

The Sunday evening fellowship hosted a retreat in the spring, which I attended. It was an awesome and powerful time where I sensed the Lord's presence so strongly. I was exposed to my first foot washing on that retreat. Jesus washed His disciples' feet. I had read about it, but I didn't know how powerful it was. We were instructed to "wait on the Lord" and be led by His

Spirit to see whose feet He would have us wash. As I was praying silently to the Lord, Pastor Dan Duis approached me to wash my feet. He prayed over me as he carried out the task, and he told me he also felt like he had a word for me from the Lord. My new church believed God would and could speak to us through others, and I agreed with them because I had seen it demonstrated, and it had been very real to me. People had spoken prophetically to me "from God" things they had no way of knowing. They had been accurate, and I had seen the things they spoke about become a reality.

"My daughter, fear not, I will always be your first love," Dan told me, saying what he sensed he heard from God on my behalf.

I started laughing because I had prayed silently about my relationship with Bob. God had answered me publicly, and no one had a clue what it all meant except God and me. Dan's prophetic word confirmed for me that I could love a man and still keep the Lord as my first love. I didn't share these things with Dan because I didn't know what Bob's feelings for me were. I just told Dan that I had prayed about something specific, and God had answered my prayer through the word Dan had been faithful to share with me.

At one of our fellowship meetings in May, the leadership let the group know that they were going to be taking a large group of teens from the church to Winchester, Virginia, in July to attend a Christian conference consisting of good teaching from multiple Bible teachers, Christian bands would be performing throughout the weekend, and vendors would be selling their wares. Dan asked that any of us willing to serve as leaders for the teens attending the conference to see him at the end of the meeting. Those of us who expressed an interest were told that as we got closer to July, our specific duties would be explained, and the leadership would make sure we were ready and prepared. We were also given the dates of the conference so we could arrange time off from our jobs, if necessary, with plenty of advance notice.

I was beginning to meet a lot of Bob's friends, as he had weekly band practice with Brent, the guy he rented a room from. They played with a couple of other guys named Richard and Chris. All of them were married except Bob and me. I hung out with their wives while the band practiced, and I found my time with these women who had known the Lord for several years very encouraging.

I kept pretty busy with work, church, and attending band practice as often as possible until July came. By then, I had been more fully prepared through the fellowship for what I would be doing with the teens at the conference.

The dates for the conference finally arrived. The only part I was a little nervous about was that we would be sleeping in tents. I had no camping experience at all.

We arrived on Friday afternoon without incident. Once at the site, the men and some of the women in the group made quick work of getting our tents set up. We had been told the youth all knew what was expected of them for the weekend, what was allowed and what wasn't. Once the tents were all set up, we followed the sound of music and enjoyed a wonderful Christian concert that night. It was fun and very uplifting to be around so many like-minded people. The youth were having a fantastic time as well.

On Saturday night, when everyone was off at the evening's conference, Bob asked me to go for a walk with him. And what man could resist me that night? After being in the humidity all day and having no opportunity for a shower, I was drenched in sweat and was embarrassed by the odor coming from my body. My hair was frizzy, and my face was sunburned, making my freckles seem all the more pronounced.

Bob stopped walking and turned to face me.

"Rita, I need to ask you an important question?" he said.

"What is it?" I asked.

"Do you think God is calling us to get married?" he asked.

"I believe He is calling us to get married," I replied.

"Then will you marry me, Rita Roth?" he asked.

"Yes, I will marry you, Bob Newell."

He smiled and drew me into his arms and kissed me tenderly. We stood in the quiet of the night, embracing for several minutes. We both felt a sense of joy and happy expectation.

We walked back to his tent and he got his guitar. He sang me a song, one that he had written to the Lord.

I called Ma Sunday morning and let her know that Bob had proposed. She excitedly congratulated me and told me how happy she was for us, and she said she knew the Lord had good things in store for us.

Bob later shared with me that he had been asking God for a wife since shortly after being saved. He hadn't considered me because I was his good friend and "not his type" when it came to girlfriend material, but sensed God asking him, "What about Rita?" Bob said, "I don't think so, Lord. I don't love her like that." He wrestled in prayer over the idea for several months as he didn't "feel in love with me" but felt like God was prompting him to consider me as an option. Bob said when he woke up on Sunday morning--after saying yes to God's idea of me for a life partner and then asking me to marry him-- he felt an incredible sense of peace. He told me he hadn't had that "peace" the whole time he was wrestling in prayer about the "who" for a wife, but the peace that now resided deep within him was his confirmation he was moving in the right direction. He had stepped out in faith, believing God knew better than he did who would be a good wife for him, and he woke up with those "feelings of love" that he had lacked previously.

After the proposal, we used our time driving back and forth to church and Sunday night fellowship to get to know more about one another. We talked about our lives before Christ and some of the regrettable choices we had made regarding drugs and relationships. I told him about my family and the abuses I had suffered and my life in foster homes and at my grandmother's. I told him I had been married before and told him about my life with Dave and how and why it had ended. He described what life had been like growing up in his household and some of the issues he faced in school.

"There's one more thing you need to know about me," I said during one of those conversations. "I've been told I might not be able to have children. I feel like it's only fair for you to know that's a real possibility. It made me really sad when they told me even though at the time, I wasn't sure if I would ever meet a man I would want to have kids with. Well, that has all changed since I met you, and I would love to be able to have children together, but I'm not sure it's possible."

"We'll cross that bridge when we come to it," he replied. "We can only take the next step in front of us. I'm glad you told me. It will just be something else we need to pray about."

Chapter 20

New Beginnings

Word had reached Pastor Derrel of our engagement, and he told us he would like to schedule a premarital counseling session with us. We agreed on a date in the next couple of weeks. We would then schedule the rest of our premarital counseling with Pa and Ma Raiford, as they were both much more intimately acquainted with us. I asked if it would be a problem to have both Derrel and Dan perform the ceremony. Derrel agreed and said they would work out the details.

At our next Tuesday night fellowship group, when the announcement was made of our upcoming wedding, the matchmakers were thrilled! They were winking at each other across the room and smiling the "I knew it" smile. I felt so loved once more by this group of wonderful women as they hugged me and congratulated me! Bob was being congratulated and encouraged by the men.

We decided we would be married on March 22, 1980, at 2:00 PM Life was busy with our premarital counseling, ordering and addressing invitations, picking bridesmaids and groomsmen, selecting a cake, choosing brides-maids' dresses, and ordering flowers. I was paying for all of my expenses myself. I found a beautiful dress in a thrift shop that fit me like a glove, and it cost only $40.00. Ma Raiford told me she and Pa had talked, and they would take care of all the expenses associated with the reception afterward as a wedding present to us. She took a huge burden off of me, and we were so grateful for the generous gift!

In our premarital session with Derrel, he didn't mince any words. He said once we got married, divorce was not an option for us because we were believers. He asked if we agreed. We both did. I am pretty sure he felt the need to discuss this issue because of my previous divorce. He went on to describe difficult circumstances we might face and asked each of us how we would resolve the problems that we would surely face. It was a sobering session, but I think it was good for us to consider things we hadn't even thought about in all the excitement.

Bob said I needed to meet his parents. I agreed, so he called them and invited them for dinner one evening when Brent and Diane would be out for the evening. We agreed we wouldn't say anything right away about the upcoming wedding. I felt they needed to get to know me a little first. I was so nervous about cooking dinner for them.

Bob had introduced all of us, and we were seated around the table enjoying dinner when Bob's dad asked him what was new. Bob blurted out that he and I were getting married in March. You should have seen the shocked looks on their faces! I was a stranger! His mother started crying and calling him her baby!

Great first meeting with the family! I was just shaking my head. I couldn't believe he had told them so abruptly after we agreed not to say anything right away. We somehow got through the rest of the meal. Bob and his father talked about God and the Bible quite a bit. We said our awkward goodbyes. They were still digesting the news.

"Why in the world did you tell them tonight when we talked about waiting?" I asked as soon as they left.

"They wanted to know what's new. Getting married is what's new," he shrugged, smiling at me.

Bob and I went out to dinner on my birthday with Brent and Diane. Bob had a present for me. I tried not to show my disappointment as I took the box because it was way too big to be the hoped-for engagement ring. Instead, it was a stuffed mama monkey with her arms wrapped around her baby. He told me to take the baby out of the mama's arms, so I did. The baby monkey had a diamond engagement ring on one of its paws. The ring was beautiful, and it fit perfectly! Afterward, we all went out to see the movie Fiddler on the Roof, one of my favorites to this day. What a wonderful birthday! What a wonderful surprise!

In the cold days of December, we wondered aloud why we had picked a day in March for the wedding! It was so far away, and we both were getting impatient for the day to be here. We had agreed on a date early in spring as our day of new beginnings. I felt it was significant. We would just have to be patient.

We spent more time with Bob's family, and they were warming up to me. I liked them. I met his only brother and his wife and little girl. They were expecting their second child about a month after the wedding. We watched a lot of football together, and it was a good way to get to know them and see how they interacted with one another.

I took Bob to meet Mama McQuaide and some of my mother's brothers and sisters. We enjoyed our visit with them very much.

Our wedding day finally came. The wedding was a beautiful ceremony. My brother, Little Ed, and one of my younger sisters attended with her husband, as well as Mama McQuaide and several members of my mother's family and some of their children were there. I was blessed and somewhat surprised that so many from my family had come. Mama sat on the front row with Ma and Pa Raiford. Bob's parents, brother and sister-in-law, and their daughter were there on the big day. Many from the home group and the Sunday evening fellowship were there, and several people from our church.

Pa Raiford gave me away, which was very special. While we had communion together as our first meal, a few worship songs were played and sung by a friend, Dwayne, from the Tuesday home group. Pastors Derrel and Dan laid hands on us and invited any elders in attendance to come forward and join them as they prayed for us. Our vows were taken before God, and the day held everything I had hoped for.

We were not going to take a honeymoon because of financial constraints, but Pa talked with Bob and said it was important for us to get away by ourselves for a few days. Someone paid for a hotel for our first night, and someone else gave us a week at a cabin on the Tappahannock River near the Chesapeake Bay. It was chilly and windy and rained a lot, but the cabin was located in an area that was quite beautiful and peaceful. We enjoyed some wonderful seafood meals at the local restaurants and enjoyed browsing in the shops in the downtown area.

We returned home to a one-bedroom apartment we had rented. Most of our furniture was borrowed from a young lady who was staying at the Farm.

She didn't have to pay to store her things, and we didn't have to buy household goods we couldn't afford at the time.

Getting married resulted in sex becoming a regular part of my life again, and I started having flashbacks to scenes from my past when my father sexually abused me. I would often feel nauseated and very upset after intimacy. I started having nightmares. I felt like I was coming unglued. I felt really bad for Bob, as he had nothing to do with that part of my life, but it was surely affecting him now.

I prayed about my problems but couldn't get any resolution. I called Ma Raiford and talked to her about what was happening. She said she would be praying for me. I told her I was contemplating getting some counseling because I couldn't seem to settle things on my own. Ma Raiford said she would support me whatever I decided to do.

Bob was very supportive of the idea of counseling. He just wanted me to have whatever help I needed to be free from my past and those wounds. I met with a spirit-filled Christian male counselor for a season, and I felt like we were making some pretty good progress. I wasn't willing to see a counselor who didn't acknowledge the existence of God. As a result of my new way of seeing things, I felt that scripture and prayer needed to be utilized during our sessions together.

A few months into it, the counselor called to tell me we would be meeting at a new address and gave me the address, directions, and a new phone number. Initially, we had met in the basement of the home he shared with his wife and children. The basement was quiet and removed from the busy household above, and it had been fine. The new location was the first floor of a townhouse. The living room was set up like a combination office and counseling room.

My counselor didn't say anything about the reason for the move, and I failed to ask him about it right away. However, after two or three sessions, I noticed other changes that caused me concern. Something in our sessions had changed, and I couldn't quite put my finger on it. Additionally, he was no longer wearing his wedding band. I felt I had to ask why the meeting place had changed. He said he and his wife were separated, and he was filing for a divorce as she was no longer meeting his emotional needs. I asked him if the rumor I heard about him seeing one of his former patients was true. He said he didn't see what that had to do with anything, but he confirmed it was true.

I was seeing him for help with my marriage, and he was leaving his wife and children. I questioned his ability to help me since he was getting divorced. He told me he was leaving his wife because she didn't meet his emotional needs. He wasn't leaving because his wife had been unfaithful to him, and that just didn't sit right with me. And he had taken up a relationship with a patient. In my opinion and judgment, he had crossed a line that shouldn't have been crossed. With the knowledge, training, and experience he had, I didn't understand why he wasn't fighting to save his own marriage, especially with how devastating divorce is for the children and for the abandoned spouse.

I called the counselor and canceled my next appointment to let him know I wouldn't be coming back. He asked me why. I told him I just wasn't comfortable seeking counseling for my marital issues from someone who was divorcing his wife. Bob and I were having fewer problems, and I had learned some new strategies for dealing with anger, so I acknowledged Mr. Counselor had helped me before I stopped seeing him. However, if he, as a trained counselor, couldn't or wouldn't access tools to help him save his own marriage, how could I be sure he was invested in helping me save mine with the many challenges I faced?

Chapter 21

Babies, Bible School, and Fires

I had missed a couple of my monthly cycles, which was just not normal for me. I purchased a pregnancy test to see if I was pregnant. The pregnancy test was positive, and Bob and I were delighted with this surprising news.

The doctor who had removed my appendix told me I would never have children. Was he wrong? I don't think so. Shortly after getting saved, I attended a prayer meeting in Washington, D.C. with Gary and received prayer specifically for the healing of my reproductive organs. I believe the God of heaven and earth healed me, and I was and am so very grateful for His power to do so! To be entrusted with the privilege of raising a child is frightening (if you come from an abusive background) and humbling.

It was an easy pregnancy, physically. It was not easy, emotionally. I got into my second trimester and was shown pictures of the stages of a developing baby in the womb for the first time in my life. I realized how developed my baby had been when I had the abortion eleven years earlier. With this new knowledge, I became overwhelmed with guilt, remorse, and regret.

I was also really angry with everyone who had encouraged me to have the procedure. In my estimation, they should have found another alternative for me. They thought they were helping me get rid of a problem when what they did was cause problems for me that I would have to face in my future.

From this place of grief, I located the doctor's office that had been involved with my abortion. The nurse took a message, and I had to wait for the doctor to call me back. The doctor who came on the line told me he was looking over my chart and wondered why I was having second thoughts about something I had done eleven years earlier. I explained that I was in my second trimester of pregnancy and seeing pictures for the first time in my life showing the stages of development of an unborn baby. I felt sure that if I had seen pictures like that before having the abortion, I would never have agreed to the procedure.

"Why didn't someone show me pictures and explain things to me so I could have made an educated decision instead of an uninformed one?" I asked him.

He encouraged me not to be so hard on myself. I was "judging" a fifteen-year-old who had been in crisis and foster care and not surrounded by family who knew and loved me (he obviously didn't know anything about my family) to help me explore all the options available to me. At this moment, I realized people had been making "clinical" decisions about what was best for me and had not meant me any harm. They helped the best way they knew how, with my given circumstances. The doctor acknowledged that this was a huge issue for me, but he advised me to put it on the back burner until I gave birth and had gotten more comfortable with my role as a mother. He said it was really important for me to be calm and at peace as much as possible during my pregnancy. He said babies in the womb were really sensitive to what was going on with their mothers. He said being upset and angry could be harmful to my unborn child. He recommended that after my baby was born, I should seek counseling if I still found myself upset and troubled by my memories surrounding the abortion.

Bob and I both thought that was good advice, so I prayed about it and asked the Lord for grace to set it aside for a season. I would tackle it when I wasn't carrying another life within me, and I wasn't so vulnerable myself.

We had our first child two and a half years after we got married and named her Katharine Anne. We gave her Ma Raiford's first name and Bob's mom's middle name. We called our little redhead Katie. She was a delightful and easy (convenient) child and began sleeping through the night at one month of age. I quit my job about a month before she was born, as Bob and I had agreed I would be a stay-at-home mother.

I had done quite a bit of reading before giving birth and thought it would help me be more prepared for all the things I didn't know about raising a baby. But when I looked into that little girl's beautiful eyes and held her in my arms, I was overwhelmed and scared because her life depended on my knowing what I was doing. I was so grateful for Ma Raiford and for a supportive doctor's office when Katie was born because I didn't know much about taking care of a newborn. I know a lot of women who have turned to their own mothers during this vulnerable time, and I was sad that I didn't have that option. Ma Raiford patiently answered my questions, as did one of the nurses at the pediatrician's office. Our Tuesday night Bible study was full of young and experienced mothers who also offered their support and encouragement.

Katie was almost three years old when we moved to upstate New York so Bob could attend a Bible school that had been recommended to him. I was seven months pregnant with our second child. I had no problems with my first pregnancy, but with the second, my blood pressure was elevated, and I also had gestational diabetes. I took no medicine for the blood pressure and was on a diet for diabetes, which helped to control my glucose levels.

Sarah was born in September, about two weeks after her dad started school and 10 days after Katie's third birthday. She was fine while we were in the hospital, but when I got her home, she was crying a lot, sleeping little, and nursing every couple of hours. It was exhausting, and Bob wasn't home much during the day because he was in school full-time and working part-time.

I called the pediatrician, and he said she wasn't getting enough milk, so I needed to start giving her formula. I was so grateful for the pediatrician I had when Katie was a newborn and all the knowledge that he shared with me about breastfeeding. Armed with what I learned from him, I disregarded the new pediatrician's advice to put her on formula. I knew he was wrong about her not getting enough milk. She was in cloth diapers and wetting a minimum of fifteen a day. Some people suggested she had colic. I was not accepting that because it seemed that there is no solution; you just have to live through this unpleasant, exhausting season.

What about my baby? She had to be crying like that because something was wrong. How could I help her? I often walked her and rocked her, and I cried with her. I felt so helpless. I began researching to find other possible causes. We couldn't afford long-distance telephone calls, so I had lost access to my network of experienced mothers in Virginia. And I needed some answers quickly! A dear friend I met at our married students' home group through the Bible college would come and walk the baby for a couple of hours, so I could spend time with Katie, get things done, or just go for a walk to escape the crying for a little bit.

I was very frustrated because I knew she was crying for a reason. She was fed and dry, and I didn't know what else could be bothering her. Finally, someone suggested I get in touch with La Leche League, so I did. I was given a list of thirteen foods found to produce symptoms of colic in nursing babies. The first item on the list was milk. I was drinking Lactaid milk, as I had been diagnosed with lactose intolerance shortly after Bob and I got married. I also ate ranch salad dressing, which was milk-based. I stopped all dairy products. La Leche told me I would have to give it three or four days. On the fourth day, I couldn't believe how long Sarah slept. She must have been exhausted herself! She was a totally different baby over the next couple of weeks. After a couple of weeks of no dairy, I tried some ranch buttermilk dressing on a salad, and Sarah started crying a lot and nursing a lot again. That was the end of my experimenting. It was definitely the milk! No sense in making either of us miserable.

I thanked the Lord that Katie was three when all this was going on because it would have been completely overwhelming with a two-year-old. Katie was mature for three years old, and I explained to her that we had finally found out what was troubling her sister. I assured her she wouldn't be crying so much, and I thanked her for her patience while we sorted things out. I told her she and I could have more time together now and that it would be a lot of fun to have a little sister as Sarah got older.

I thought about my mother during this time because my grandmother said I had colic and cried all the time as an infant. My father had been in the Navy, and he was gone a lot. Cathy had a fourteen-month-old and a crying infant. Her mother had a new baby, too, so she could not really offer her much help. She must have felt very alone and frustrated. I felt compassion for her. I also knew that she didn't know about crying out to God for peace and comfort in the midst of the storm.

We met a lot of wonderful people at Bible school, and they were a real encouragement to us. We had some sweet fellowship with many new friends. Worship at church was awesome.

Even though things were better with Sarah, we lived about twenty minutes from the school and had only one car, so I was feeling pretty isolated. Bob was juggling too much for me to make arrangements during the day to have the car.

In January, right before winter break ended, I woke up in the middle of the night from a dream where I was on fire. I smelled something burning, and it had an electrical smell. I searched upstairs and downstairs but didn't see smoke anywhere. I went back upstairs and woke Bob up. He smelled it too and told me to call the neighbors who lived in the studio apartment that was attached to our home and alert them. I called them while Bob gathered Katie, and he hollered over his shoulder that he was taking her to Mrs. West's home next door. He had bundled her in her blankets because of the brutally cold weather outside but hadn't risked losing time by dressing her in warmer clothing. I called the neighbors and told them we smelled something and thought the house was on fire, and we were getting the girls out. The neighbor said she didn't smell anything in her part of the home. While I was slipping into some clothes, the neighbor called back and said the apartment was filling with smoke. She asked me to call the fire department, as they needed to get out quickly. I called the fire department and went to get Sarah across the hall. As I lifted my not quite four-month-old daughter from her crib, her room filled with smoke! I hurried out of the house with her bundled in her crib blankets and joined Bob and Katie at Mrs. West's home next door to us.

The firemen had to hack through parts of the ceiling and parts of Sarah's bedroom wall with an ax to get at the fire and to get it put completely out. They measured the creosote in the wall and told us it had been burning in the chimney behind Sarah's bedroom wall since 11:00 PM It was now 3:00 AM. The neighbors were using a wood stove in a chimney fireplace that hadn't been cleaned recently; a wood stove burns longer and hotter than a fireplace.

A fireman told me that if Sarah had been in that room for a couple of minutes longer after it began filling with smoke, we would have lost her. Her little lungs would have been overwhelmed by the volume of smoke in the air. We saw God's mighty hand of protection and thanked Him for intervening!

We called the dean of students at the Bible school, and he said we could stay with his family until we could make other arrangements. We stayed with them for a couple of days until we were notified that there was an apartment on campus we could live in until the necessary repairs were completed at our house.

When Bob went to school the next day, the faculty and students found out what had happened. They prayed for our family and specifically for Sarah during chapel, and those praying thanked the Lord for keeping us safe.

It was the only time thus far in our married lives that we had purchased renter's insurance. Bob had been praying about things with the move to New York, and he felt like, in spite of our limited finances, we should get renter's insurance along with our car insurance. We thanked God for His faithfulness to give Bob direction when he had prayed because it was also the first time we had ever needed renter's insurance.

I loved being on campus, and so did Katie. We saw people every day, and we both really enjoyed the interactions after our months of isolation. Katie, Sarah, and I often joined Bob during the chapel service. The worship was awesome, and the teaching was encouraging and challenging.

While staying in town, we learned of an apartment that would be available in July, a block from campus, and a block from the grocery store. We asked the family living there currently to give our name and number to the landlord and let him know we wanted to rent it when they moved out. That July, we found ourselves moving once again.

I was so much happier when we moved into town. The one-car limitation was not too bad when there were lots of other married students just up the block and over the hill. I was nowhere near as isolated as I had been our first year there. The house we had rented in Livonia was comfortable and spacious, and the landlord and his wife had been kind to us. Now our quarters were much smaller. The apartment was in a house that had been divided into four units. To enter it, one stepped directly into the eat-in kitchen. To the left were the bedrooms and one had to pass through one to get to the other. The bathroom was off of the kitchen, and the living room to the right of the entry. There was a basement for the washer and dryer and a huge back yard set back from the street.

Bob could walk to classes in the morning, and I could take the car for errands or appointments and be back in the early afternoon when he would need it to go to work. The grocery store, library, and a playground were all within walking distance of our new apartment.

Bob had found a lady in town who wanted a lot of work done on her house. He wasn't making what he used to make, but God took care of us. Our church back in Virginia was paying for his schooling. One of the families there sent us $50.00 a month, which was a tremendous blessing. Bob had a mailbox on campus, and he often found envelopes containing cash that had been donated anonymously.

At the apartment, we had another good landlord. If one of the units became empty, I would show the unit for him. That way, he wouldn't have to come into town unless someone was seriously interested. He lived about thirty minutes away, so it was a good arrangement.

Bob mowed the lawn in exchange for a fixed rent that didn't go up once in the eight years we rented from him. I ended up with a filing cabinet, some parts catalogs, and a dictation machine in our living room and got paid for doing some occasional typing for the landlord. We were often unable to pay the rent in the winter, as Bob didn't have much work. We let the landlord know and told him as soon as work picked back up in the spring, we would prioritize getting the rent caught up. He worked with us and never pressured us. And we always got caught back up in the spring.

Right across the yard, in the next house, lived an older couple. The husband had been a teacher at the Bible school and now owned a local pizza place with another guy. His wife was very good to the girls and would ask Katie to come over sometimes and do special craft projects with her. I ended up doing a bit of typing for the pizza business as well.

Also, after the first year of Bob's schooling, we decided he was going to take only a maximum of nine credit hours until he graduated. The school discouraged that and thought he would give up and not finish. They even talked to him about it. He told them he had to do what was best for his family, and we would be a lot less stressed if we took it at a pace we could handle since he was our only provider as well. We attended a Bible study made up of other married students from the Bible school, and they openly shared that they were stressed, and so were their families, with the pace of things. We figured if we could slow down the pace, there would be less stress.

One afternoon, I got the girls bundled up to run errands in Rochester.

"Where are we going, Mom?" Katharine asked.

"I need to pick up some hujamaquias," I told her.

"What's a hujamaquia?" she asked.

"A hujamaquia is like a thingamajig," I said. "When I'm distracted and can't remember the name of something, I call it a hujamaquia. In this case, hujamaquias are filters for the vaporizer. I made up the word hujamaquia because I think it sounds better than thingamajig. If you don't know what something is called, you could call it a hujamaquia. If you describe the thing to me, we can figure out what the real word for it is."

Sarah fell asleep during the twenty-minute ride. We found a parking spot nice and close to the store. Katie suggested we leave Sarah in the van that we had recently been given. I thought about it for a minute; it was tempting. Then I told her it was never, ever a good idea to leave children in a car. You just don't know what might happen, I told her as I woke Sarah up to take her into the store.

We were in the store for about ten minutes before one of the salesclerks started yelling that if anyone had parked next to the orange van in the lot, they should move their car as quickly as possible. He went on to explain that the van was engulfed in flames, and the other car would be next if it was not moved. We walked up to the front of the store so we could look out the large window.

"As I was saying, Katie, you never know what might happen, so you just don't leave your kids alone in the car," I reiterated.

We stood there looking at our van. The whole front end was on fire, and flames leapt out from under the hood. I was horrified at the thought that I had considered even for a moment, leaving Sarah asleep in her car seat for convenience sake and amazed that for the second time in a relatively short time frame, Sarah had been spared from the dangers of a second fire.

I used the store telephone to make arrangements for someone to come and pick us up. Once the firemen put the fire out, I was able to retrieve the girls' car seats from the still smoldering van.

That evening as we said our prayers before eating our dinner, we took a few moments to thank God again for His mighty hand of protection when we didn't even know we had need of it. The van could just as easily have caught fire as I was driving the girls to the store. My usual response to any emergency was sheer panic. I was so grateful we weren't in that van when it burst into flames. I don't know if I would have had the presence of mind to safely get the girls out, and I was glad I hadn't had to find out!

Of course, over the next several weeks, our friends and acquaintances at the Bible school made jokes about how we must really be "on fire" for the Lord. The van caught on fire about three months after we had the house fire.

A couple of months later, Bob and I worked out a weekend where I could go to the Abbey of the Geneseo, where one could have private retreats. With my increased responsibilities after having Sarah, I found I was dealing with a lot of anger, and I was not as patient as I would have liked. I felt a need to get away and seek the Lord about the unrest and turmoil in my heart.

I had a refreshing time just spending concentrated time reading the Bible and praying about things without having to juggle my normal responsibilities. I left there with a hopeful attitude.

I stopped at the local grocery store to pick up a few things on my way home. A woman I knew from the Bible college came up to me in the produce section and said she was so glad everyone was okay. I had no idea what she was talking about. As I stood in the checkout line behind a man from the Bible school, he turned to me and said he was really glad no one had come to harm. I felt like I was on an adventure in the Twilight Zone. What were these people talking about? I could have asked but just wanted to get home to Bob and the girls as I felt alarmed by their comments.

I got home and audibly sighed with relief as I saw my family was safe. I told Bob about the strange comments I had heard at the grocery store. He told me to call one of our babysitters from the Bible school and see if they could watch the girls for about an hour. He said he would explain everything once the sitter got there.

In about fifteen minutes, one of the girls from school came, and Bob told me to come with him. We got in the car, and he drove us to the house he had been working on for months. I couldn't believe my eyes as we pulled into the driveway, and I stared at what remained of the home. There had obviously been a fire, and the top floor of the home had been consumed. It had been a historic home in the community with a captain's watch on the top of the house. That was all gone.

Bob explained to me that the man who had recently begun to help with work on the house was stripping off the old paint with a heat gun and putty knife when something behind the wood burst into flames. The captain's watch set on top of a cement base and trapped the fire inside, making it difficult for the firemen to put out the fire. The firemen thought Pete had accidentally caught a bird's nest on fire, and the fire spread quickly, consuming the top floor of the home. Pete had been able to warn everyone inside, so they escaped unharmed.

We walked through the house with tears streaming down our faces. The lady who owned it had provided Bob with enough work to keep the bills caught up and food on the table. There was an overwhelming sense of loss, even though it was not our house. The owner had conveyed to Bob when he started the job what her goals were with the remodeling, and there had been a lot of satisfaction for both of them as the project progressed. Every improvement he had made was destroyed in the fire!

We stood in the midst of the ruined home, crying and praying. We thanked God for protecting the people who lived there but cried out for an understanding of what was going on and how we were to move forward. We prayed for the owner and her family. We prayed for the young man who had inadvertently started the fire. There was no way he could have known what was going to happen.

The owner moved in with her sister, who lived in the neighborhood. She was very gracious and kind to us in spite of the loss she had suffered and the inconvenience of being displaced. She actually worked with her insurance company and a builder to design a new home to be built on the site. Though she lost just about everything, she was able to preserve the beautiful cherry staircase from the original home and use it in the new home.

People from church and the Bible school were very supportive and encouraging during this difficult time. No one made jokes with this latest fire about us being "on fire" for the Lord.

Bob lost his business insurance as the result of the fire, and he ended up going to work for a factory in the area where many of the other students worked. He had to work some odd hours, but he always did what was necessary to take care of us and our obligations.

Bob continued to declare God's goodness and faithfulness to us in spite of the difficulties and suffering we had to endure in our lives. He was a wonderful example of pressing into God and seeking Him in the midst of the trials. He didn't turn away or curse God for the hardships. He said we had to find out what He was after in our hearts and that we should worship and praise Him in spite of our circumstances.

Chapter 22

Counseling and Writing

I struggled with anger on a daily basis because I had been sweeping all kinds of issues under the rug, as I had no idea how to deal with them. This produced bumps in the rug, which tripped me up on a regular basis. The growing issues under the rug were the things I had to get at; the anger was just a symptom of the cancer growing in me fed by hatred, bitter thoughts, and an unforgiving spirit.

I couldn't know true freedom in my "present" because I was bound to the memories and pain of my past. I found it impossible to grow in my relationship with God as my Father. My experiences thus far taught me fathers were dangerous and couldn't be trusted. There were so many unresolved issues in my heart that I found it difficult to have an unhindered relationship with my husband and our children. I didn't want to hurt my family with anger and rage. I had firsthand knowledge of living with the unresolved anger and rage of another person, and it was the cause of most of the problems I was experiencing in my day to day life. Since my past issues were unresolved, that seemed to be where I was heading, and it terrified me.

When I had only one child, I felt like I could handle most of my responsibilities. I would sometimes deal with intense PMS symptoms, but I just figured that was part of being a woman. I wasn't overly concerned about it as it was brief and passed. I also established strategies for dealing with my period. I kept a chart that reflected three months at a time so I could track when I was most likely to have "symptoms." This was so I could be proactive by making sure I got enough rest and avoiding excess sugar and coffee, which probably exacerbated my symptoms.

But when I had my second child, I felt more overwhelmed. It seemed to me there were always things that had been left undone. I never felt caught up with my responsibilities. I also felt like the PMS symptoms were worse and found myself losing my temper more often and overreacting to situations. It had nothing to do with my sweet, new baby. Once my responsibilities increased, I could no longer tell myself that I was in control. Being in control before my second child was born had only been an illusion.

I found myself yelling a lot more often, and I didn't like it, and the girls definitely didn't like it. I was careful about what I yelled. I didn't call them names or deliberately ridicule them. However, I would say things like, "Why can't you be more careful?" if they spilled something. But I was yelling and not discussing. When I found myself overreacting to situations at home, I started taking a "timeout." I explained to my girls who were older at that time that I needed to take a timeout and spend a few minutes with God. I told them they hadn't done anything wrong, but I was having a problem and needed time with God to help find a resolution. They were to be on their beds for a few minutes with books until I came back out, and they weren't to bother one another for any reason. This worked really well, and I usually needed only about five to ten minutes to get myself under control. I also would go in the bathroom and turn on the fan and yell and holler into a towel when I needed to let things out. This was a safe vent when I felt like I was exploding with anger! It didn't take very long and was a quicker fix than my "timeout" method. I usually ended up crying afterward without being able to put my finger on exactly what was troubling me!

It seemed impossible for me to maintain a peaceful atmosphere in the home because I knew I was overreacting. Even though I was able to establish some of my own strategies for dealing with anger, I also feared I was becoming more and more like my angry mother. I prayed about it and felt like I needed to get some counseling.

I met with Pastor Bob Sorge from our church to let him know I was going to be pursuing some counseling for unresolved past issues in my life. I gave him some general background information about the emotional and verbal abuse.

He asked me to be more specific about the verbal abuse.

I told him, "She was constantly telling me I was ugly and that one of the meanings of my name was ugly."

Pastor Bob said, "Let's see what God has to say about your appearance, okay? Genesis 1:27 says, "God created mankind in His own image. In the image of God, He created them." In Psalm 139:13, it says, 'For You created my inmost being; You knit me together in my mother's womb. I praise You because I am fearfully and wonderfully made; Your works are wonderful, I know that full well.' Rita, your mother may have told you that you were ugly, but that doesn't mean it's true. What does God's word say about you? It says you were created in His image and you are fearfully and wonderfully made. That's the truth about your appearance so, she lied to you. Who will you believe? Your mother or the Lord? As to your name, Rita, it doesn't mean ugly or stupid. It means pearl. A pearl is a beautiful and highly prized gem. Your mother had it wrong on all counts."

"I will believe the Lord," I replied.

Pastor Bob said, "You said she called you stupid all the time. 1 Corinthians 2:16 says, 'we have the mind of Christ.' That includes you. In 2 Timothy 1:7, it says, "God hath not given us the spirit of fear; but of power, of love, and of a sound mind." James 1:5 says, "If any of you lacks wisdom, you should ask God, Who gives generously to all without finding fault, and it will be given to you." So the wisdom of the Lord is available to you if you ask for it. I see nothing in God's word to indicate that you are stupid, so again, your mother lied to you. "

"She also said I would never amount to anything," I said.

Pastor Bob said, "God's word says, "For I know the plans I have for you, declares the Lord, plans to prosper you and not to harm you, plans to give you hope and a future." That verse is found in Jeremiah 29:11."

"She said I would rot in hell," I said.

"He who believes in Him shall not be judged," and "For God so loved the world that he gave his one and only son, that whoever believes in him shall not perish but have eternal life." That's in John 3:15-16," Pastor Bob said.

Pastor Bob prayed for me that I would be able to reject the things my mother said to me as untrue based on what we could see in the Bible and that I would be able to view myself as God saw me, and not through the lens of my broken and damaged mother.

He asked me if I would like to set up a follow-up appointment to talk about some other issues. I thanked him for his willingness but told him I had been praying about how to move forward and that I felt God had directed me to set up counseling with Judy, one of the teachers at the Bible school. Pastor Bob told me his door was always open if I needed him.

As we concluded our time together, I felt like a huge weight had been lifted off of me. I felt light, carefree, and happy even. I had been told lies throughout my childhood. Now I knew the truth, and it was a very liberating experience. I felt like skipping out of his office.

Judy Hays, who taught counseling and pastoral care at the college, gave free pastoral counseling to people in the campus community. I heard that she offered a listening ear, prayer, and a shoulder to cry on. I decided to go see her. I needed help making peace with my past, so I could move forward. I called Judy and scheduled my first appointment.

At that appointment, I shared my abuse history with Judy, throwing out several experiences I had endured. I told her my biggest concern was the anger that seemed to always be just below the surface. I told her I used to be able to control the anger, but it was erupting all the time now. Judy encouraged me to beat the chair with her briefcase. I told her I wasn't mad at her chair or the briefcase and that I had been exposed to such "therapies" in the foster homes in which I had lived, and it had never seemed beneficial to me. I explained my strategies to her for coping day to day but let her know I was looking for resolution and freedom. Judy said she would ask some other counselors she knew if they had suggestions for dealing with serious anger issues. She would let me know what she learned.

When I met with Judy the following week, she said that counselors at Agape Counseling in Rochester recommended writing, as it had proved to be a great outlet for many of their clients. She suggested I choose a troubling memory and write a letter to one of my parents about that memory and what I was feeling and thinking. These letters would never be mailed; they were only for the purpose of helping me vent and heal. I should dump whatever emotions were stirring within me onto that paper and not censor my thoughts or words. We would discuss the letter at our next session.

I was encouraged to pray and tell God I forgave the one inflicting the abuse for the actions they had taken and the words they had said to me in the memory I had addressed. I was also supposed to ask Him to forgive them. I was to ask for forgiveness for myself for harboring anger and hate and rage and allowing those negative emotions to dwell in my own heart. This would be one of the hardest parts of the process.

Judy explained that forgiveness didn't make the abuse alright; the harm my parents had inflicted upon me was clearly wrong, and nothing would change that fact. There was no explaining or justifying their behavior. Judy said forgiveness would provide a spiritual release to the perpetrators and to me. What did that mean? I'm not sure, but I had not completely forgiven Cathy and Edward. The condition of my heart and the anger showed me that I still had unresolved issues to address. I was bound to them and to my past by the hatred and bitterness deep inside of me.

Judy's recommendation made me both hopeful and excited. I believed that she had suggested something that might work. I didn't want my unresolved issues hurting my little girls or my husband. They had not wronged me and should not feel the brunt of my wrath over a "cup of spilled milk."

In foster homes and in meeting with shrinks over the years, I had been exposed to a lot of people's ideas and thoughts regarding what might help with inner healing. I found most of what was suggested only confused the issues for me and had not given me the resolution I so desperately needed. Judy's suggestion was great because I loved writing, and I wouldn't be hurting anyone by writing letters and destroying them! In all the years of counseling I had received, writing had never been suggested as a way to deal with memories and pain.

I chose to write my letters when the girls were in bed, and Bob was out visiting friends. I used our living room and closed the door. We had kept a "Do Not Disturb" sign from a hotel, and I hung it on the outside doorknob when I was praying and writing. Most of my writing sessions ended with me crying, and I wasn't quiet. I played worship music in the kitchen, so if the girls got up to use the restroom, they would hear the music instead of me.

As I readied myself to write, it didn't take long for a memory to surface. I saw in my mind's eye a horrible scene from my childhood. In this particular memory, my mother was holding a lit cigarette against the flesh of my arm. She would wait until she saw the smoke rising from the burning skin to move the cigarette to a new spot, burning me up and down the length of my arm. The acrid smell of my burning flesh was nauseating. I remembered the overwhelming sense that I was going to throw up, but I had to swallow the burning flood of bile. There was no telling what she would do to me if I actually threw up. There was no doubt that whatever she did would mean enduring more pain. As the memory came, I scribbled out everything I saw and thought and felt and smelled. I was livid about being so mistreated and abused by my mother. I wrote that letter to her, directing the pent-up rage I felt towards her. I "dumped" everything into the letter, and I cried throughout the exercise. Once I finished writing the letter, I began to pray for my mother by name, asking the Lord to heal the wounds in her heart that caused her to hurt me. I prayed, "I forgive her, Lord, for burning my arm over and over. I forgive her. Please help me to truly forgive her and not harbor hatred in my heart. Please don't hold this against her, Lord."

I discovered that writing was a powerful weapon for dealing with the pain and trauma of my childhood. I could say whatever I needed to say, and it was an incredible and effective way to vent years of buried, negative emotions. Writing helped me define things that were without definition to me in times past. Writing opened a door inside me that had been slammed shut and locked for over thirty years.

I had been silenced and dismissed by those who had great influence and power over me. They would take my words and twist them and say I had said something I had not said. So speaking words often resulted in even more pain. The Lord used writing to help me find my voice and freed me from years of silence.

The writing process has helped me to face and resolve destructive and dangerous emotions. It opened the door for me to forgive my parents in a way that I hadn't been able to before because writing allowed me to safely explore and express the turmoil and pain in my heart. Writing has helped me to deal with emotions I feared and ran from and tried to turn off. They were the same emotions ruling my father and mother when they inflicted pain upon me. I faced my demons through my writing.

As a result of this discovery, I spent time at the end of most days with my journal. I made it my habit for many years. When I had finished my daily writing, I would feel as if I had faced something and dealt with it on a level I didn't yet fully understand. I actually began sleeping better because journaling before bedtime had a cleansing effect on me.

At one session, Judy asked me to quiet myself and allow a memory to come. The ugly memories surfaced when bidden to do so. Then Judy suggested that I picture the Lord in the memory, and she wanted to know what He was doing.

She had pushed a button! I was so angry seeing Jesus in a memory, where both my parents were beating me because He did nothing to stop them or to stop the abuse. How could He be a good God and allow them to hurt me over and over again? Why hadn't He done something to help me? Why hadn't He rescued me? Judy's question brought me face to face with the reality that I was angry with God because He didn't do what I thought He should've done in the situation.

My weekly sessions with Judy left me feeling restless and on edge. All of the emotions rising to the surface frightened me terribly because I felt like I was losing all sense of control.

A few months after I started counseling with Judy, I talked with Bob about maybe not going back because everything was all stirred up. I told him I felt like I was in worse shape than when I started. I feared my emotions would push me over the edge, and I wasn't sure I would be able to recover.

He said that was only an illusion because I had been successfully sweeping my problems under the rug for years and avoiding anything that was even remotely painful. Bob said I wasn't in better shape before I started counseling. I was living in denial then. He encouraged me, saying that it did seem worse for now, but that was because I was finally facing things I had been unwilling to face before. He reassured me by reminding me that true freedom was my goal, and I would be able to finally close the door on the past because it would no longer have a hold on me if I persevered in this rough season. My dear husband told me he was proud of me and that I was one of the most courageous people he had ever met!

So, I continued with the counseling. Judy and I had several sessions discussing letters I had written to my mother about many different memories. We prayed at the end of our sessions.

At the end of one of our sessions, Judy and I were praying about one of the memories, and I saw the Lord in the memory even as Cathy and Edward were hurting me and cursing at me. He was weeping with me. He didn't direct their actions or their lives. They were not robots. They, like all people, had been given the gift of free will. If they were going to hurt me, He couldn't turn them off or put them on pause to protect me from pain. He was good in spite of what my parents had done to me.

Chapter 23

A Letter to Edward

At the end of one of our sessions, Judy insisted we start dealing with the issues of my father. She told me she knew tackling those memories was going to be very hard, but it was necessary. She said it was time to start writing my letters specifically to him. That was my homework; to be completed before we met again.

Judy encouraged me to really open up my heart during the process and to not shut things down if it became too painful. Don't filter it, she said, just dump it. When I was finished with the letter, I was to take time to pray to God, asking Him to forgive my father for what he had done and asking Him to cleanse me of the anger and rage and hate I had deep in my heart.

The next weekend, Bob took the girls to a friend's house for an extended visit and said he would be gone for several hours. He told me to get my homework done, assured me of his love, and said he would be praying for me.

Again, Dear Reader, you may want to skip the rest of this chapter because it contains specifics that will be upsetting to read, but I retell these details because I want other women who have experienced sexual abuse to know that I do understand as I too suffered those abuses. I have struggled even writing about this memory. I was told my first version was way too vague, and then my next version I was told was way too graphic. I tried to find the balance between the two with you in mind, my Reader. I want us to be able to help one another to a place of complete healing.

As it turns out, I actually wrote the letter to Edward on his birthday, Saturday, August 22, 1988. God did promise me my life would end victoriously, and I would walk in freedom and peace and great joy. I believed Him, and that is why I faced the horrible memories and wrote a letter to Edward, detailing the multiple ways he had violated me over the years. The time he took me from the safety of my classroom and the horrible things he did to me when he got me home was the focus of the letter. Suffice it to say, my father forced me to perform oral sex on him, and he performed oral sex on me. I brushed my teeth afterward, but my mouth never felt clean again for years. I am purposely sparing you the details, Dear Reader, but know that I was haunted by the memory for years after it occurred. As I was writing this book, I realized I had not brought this particular memory to the Lord to seek His healing for the wounding it caused because the incident stirred up so much shame, I just wasn't willing to confront it.

I wrote several pages, spilling the rage and anger that churned inside me onto the paper. I cried and yelled and carried on, trying to sort through the overwhelming pain--for pain was the real issue here. The anger was real, but it was like a shield protecting me from the pain. Anger was easier to face than the pain inside. I don't know why; maybe anger made me feel more in control. Writing that letter had me completely stirred up, and I couldn't forgive him as I had been instructed.

"Father God help me to be willing to forgive him," I prayed. "I can't make the forgiveness real. Right now, I really don't want to forgive him. I am sorry."

Tears streamed down my face. I was broken, and no one could make me whole. I could not remember a time in my life when I had felt whole. I had been broken from early childhood.

"Why? Why?" I screamed. "How can someone do things like that to a young child? Edward was supposed to protect me. That's what fathers do, right? Instead, he used me and hurt me in such a way that I'm not sure I will be able to recover. Why didn't anyone protect me? I couldn't protect myself; I was only a little girl. I had no resources. Oh, Lord, please, help me! My heart hurts so badly. How can I make it stop? It's smothering me; it's crushing me. There's pain and heaviness and shame everywhere. I can't get away from it! I can't breathe. Please help me. I can't breathe. I am so scared!"

I was sobbing uncontrollably and rocking my body back and forth to try to comfort myself. The dam had broken, and the torrent that had been held back for so long was loosed, and I couldn't stop it. The sounds of pain and devastation thundered from deep within me and filled our living room that afternoon as I gave expression to the overwhelming mix of emotions. I felt like I was sinking below the surface as years of suppressed emotions burst to the surface. It was like being in that rock quarry all over again. I was fully submerged and didn't know if I could or would make it back to the top for air. There was nothing I could grab to pull myself up above the darkness and despair.

I did not share the memory or the letter with Judy. I was filled with shame and had never been able to tell anyone what he had done to me that day he took me from the safety of my classroom. It was difficult for me to discuss the sexual abuse and I only remember barely scratching the surface with Judy.

After writing that letter to Edward and that gut-wrenching evening crying and praying, I felt like I needed a break from counseling. I didn't know if it was possible to make peace with that memory and to really be able to set it aside and move on. But I didn't want to look at it anymore or think about it at that time.

I was definitely in a better place emotionally, mentally, and spiritually as a result of the time, I had spent with Judy. I was rarely having nightmares anymore. I wasn't overreacting to everything. I was able to enjoy intimacy with my husband without the past abuses of my father intruding into our time together. I had new tools for dealing with anger and stress. I was more at peace.

During the time I spent with Judy, we had dealt with a lot of memories I had never been able to deal with before. I felt I had been helped by her significantly as a result. But we didn't address everything, and, like the layers of an onion, there were still untouched, hidden layers that would need to be addressed in the future.

Chapter 24

Finding Freedom in God

Praying and connecting with the Lord daily helped me live my life more in keeping with the scripture. He helped me nurture my girls and be a good wife and mother. He helped me keep my focus in the right place. Connecting to God and trying to stay connected to Him had a calming effect on me.

Bob had built a spectacular playhouse for the girls in our yard. Adults could stand up inside, even though they might need to duck down a bit to enter. It even had electricity. On warmer nights in the summer, the girls slept out there in sleeping bags.

I started to use the playhouse for private devotions in the mornings, even in winter. I would bundle up in my long down winter coat and turn on a portable heater I had put out there to take the brutal chill out of the air. I had some wonderful times with the Lord in the playhouse.

Over the passing months, I felt less anxious and troubled about things in our life that I couldn't really do anything about anyway. Life's problems still needed solutions, but they didn't overwhelm me like they did when I wasn't having a regular time apart with the Lord. Nothing had changed--except me! I was more comfortable with Father God following the freedom I felt after talking and praying with Judy about some difficult things. Time in God's presence was bringing peace and rest to my soul.

Our church started participating in a program called Cleansing Stream, through which I received even more healing from my past. Cleansing Stream was a series of meetings dealing with various aspects of the teachings of Jesus. It was suggested if you were living according to His word, then your life should be void of certain problems. However, if you chose not to follow His instructions, then you could bring problems upon yourself as a result of the choices made. If one was closely following His instructions and still having significant problems, then maybe one needed deliverance.

The teaching seemed very well rounded to me. We weren't looking for a demon behind every bush but rather examining our lives to see if the trouble was a result of our own choices in life--sowing and reaping, as it were. We had books to read, tapes to listen to, scriptures to research, and workbooks to complete. Husbands and wives who never prayed together, committed to praying together throughout the preparation period. We met weekly with other married couples and single people in a home setting to discuss the things we were learning. We could ask for prayer and pray for others in this supportive setting. Once we worked through the workbooks, read the books, and listened to the tapes, we would go away on a weekend retreat to address the things that didn't get resolved by other means.

The participants from our church all went to West Virginia for that retreat. We were joined by people from other churches who were going through the Cleansing Stream program. There was a team of people who had been trained in various aspects of deliverance and intercession waiting for us and eager to minister to us. It was a very loving and warm environment. During the retreat, I went up front for prayer to deal with a spirit of anger. Though a lot of my issues had improved through talking and praying, writing, and learning to forgive, there were still occasions I was overwhelmed with a rage that seemed to come from nowhere. I knew there were unresolved roots of anger in me.

When I went up for prayer against anger, the power of God hit me in such a fashion that I flew backward several feet before landing on the floor. I was unharmed. I lost my shoes as I went flying backward, even though I was wearing securely tied sneakers. Do you know how people come out of their shoes from the force involved in being in a car accident? That's what I compared it to. After members of the ministry team finished praying for me, I had to go hunt for my shoes.

Though my husband saw positive results after I went through various seasons of "counseling," he told me months later that after that night of being prayed for specifically about anger at the retreat, I wasn't the same as I had been before. There was a noticeable, significant, and lasting change. I wasn't the same and was no longer driven by unresolved anger.

When we talked with people after the retreat, many of them had testimonies of lasting changes in their lives, of walking in newfound freedoms. They told of improved relationships in their marriages and within their families. Some told of being able to reconcile with someone where the relationship had been broken for years. Many had learned the power of forgiveness and of extending it to those who didn't deserve it. (Who of us can honestly say we deserve it?) Many had added some new habits to their lives, like praying and reading the word together. They saw the fruit of their choices and were determined to be more disciplined in their approach to various aspects of their lives. We had the privilege ourselves of riding in an elevator with a woman who was terrified of elevators. She prayed the whole time, but she was able to face that fear head-on for the first time in her life.

Then our church, in an effort to make the retreats more affordable, decided to host and put together their own Spiritual Freedom Seminar, based on things we had learned through Cleansing Stream. There were a lot of people in our fellowship who couldn't take advantage of something like Cleansing Stream because of all the expenses (hotels, food, gas, babysitters) involved. Our church leaders wanted those people to have an opportunity to hear similar teaching and have prayer for areas in which they struggled. This effort proved to be beneficial and helped a lot of the people at our church.

At the first Spiritual Freedom Seminar hosted by our church, one of the leaders, Dave, approached me and asked if I would do a teaching at the seminar, sharing how the Lord had delivered me from problems with uncontrollable anger. I asked to pray about it and promised to get back to him. After praying about it for a few days, I had the sense that it was an opportunity to share what God can do for us when we yield to Him and His purposes and to testify of the incredible changes He was making in my heart. Bob agreed, so I called Dave and told him I would be willing to share my testimony on how the Lord had ministered to me. He asked me to mark the date on my calendar and told me he would look forward to it.

I worked on my preparation and prayed and asked for God's help so that His people would hear words of hope and life and truth. I prayed their hearts would be open to God as they heard my story of deliverance resulting in many new freedoms. Bob prayed with me also as I prepared, and before I went up to speak.

The Lord anointed the time, and it was one of the most precious memories I have in my walk with Him. I literally and personally felt the "wind of the Holy Spirit" blow across me before I began speaking and was immediately filled with a giddy joy. I knew this wasn't up to me, and I couldn't make anything happen. I needed Father God's help with timing and words and delivery to minister life and release hope to His people. He helped me make them laugh before I made them cry with some of my stories of abuse in my home. I felt God's anointing upon me. I felt the rivers of living water in my belly all stirred up. I felt His tangible presence as I spoke to His people. By my Lord's grace and His empowerment, I spoke words of life, hope, and truth, and peoples' lives were touched. People who had stopped believing that things could ever change had hope again. People who were afraid to speak about the horrors they had lived through for fear they wouldn't be believed would now have the courage to speak and to seek out help and prayer until they were able to walk in freedom.

I was standing up there speaking because my God had brought me through some terrible things and helped me really forgive people for the wrongs they had committed against me. I saw a lot of people crying and invited them up front for prayer. It was a privilege and an honor to be able to pray for these wounded hearts and to speak hope to them through the authority of the Holy Spirit because of His faithfulness to me. The Lord brought me to a place of wholeness, forgiveness, and deep inner peace that I had previously thought was forever out of my reach.

When we were driving home, my husband, who is a gifted teacher, gave me the best compliment ever. He told me the presentation was both linear and logical, and easy to understand. He also sensed the Lord's anointing on it. It wasn't about me; it was about God, who gave His only begotten Son to die on the cross that all might be able to walk in wholeness, truth, victory, and freedom in spite of what had been done to them by others or in spite of what they may have done to wound others. It was about the goodness and faithfulness of God.

Sharing my testimony in that setting was one of the most inspiring things I have been able to participate in so far in my Christian walk. Being able to stir up faith in someone else and get them walking with hope in their hearts again is very rewarding. Knowing that someone might have the courage to chase after God with new abandon and the freedom He offers because of my testimony was satisfying and fulfilling to me.

I was in a really good place, but my Father wasn't finished with the work He had begun in me to truly deliver me from the pains and wounds of my past. I was looking more like Jesus after all the healing and restoration He had done in me, but there were still buried hurts that would cause problems later if not resolved. I thought everything was resolved, but He, who knows the end from the beginning, knew there was more work to be done.

The Bible college my husband was attending advertised that they had a special speaker coming in from Brownsville Assembly of God in Pensacola, Florida, where the Spirit of God was apparently moving powerfully among the members of that church. His name was Ray Sell. We decided to go up on a Sunday evening to check it out. Word had obviously gotten out. We got there about ten minutes early, and it was already standing room only already.

Truly, the speaker had the anointing of God on him, and God was moving powerfully in our midst. Our church originally had him booked for a few days only but ended up extending his invitation to minister for several weeks. They also wanted him to take some time to train the church leaders in this ministry so they could continue the teaching and ministry after he left. Ray Sell was speaking in the mornings during the week to the students at the school, but the public was welcome. He was also speaking in the evenings throughout the week and twice on Sundays.

Bob and I attended a lot of the sessions. Bob was working during the day, but we took the girls to several of the evening sessions as part of our home school, and it was considered an extracurricular activity. The girls were being ministered to and learning new things about the Spirit of God. There was plenty of time for worship at the beginning of the meetings, which helped me get focused and lay aside all the distractions and concerns of the day.

One particular night, Bob stayed home to watch the girls, and I went to the meeting alone. Mike C., the pastor of the church on campus, was in charge of the meeting. He gave an encouraging and challenging word and then invited those wanting prayer to come to the altar. I felt the tug of the Holy Spirit and went up for prayer. Mike placed a hand on my forehead and prayed quietly for a couple of minutes.

Then he prayed more specifically, "Father, reveal every hidden, dark place in Rita's heart, that she might walk in the freedom You have for her. Minister to her by Your Spirit Lord, setting her free from all that binds her."

As I knelt at the altar, I saw a "movie" playing over and over in my mind, and it was the horrible memory that I had written about in the letter to my father. I felt hot, angry tears falling from my eyes, but I was crying silently at this point. I saw my father Edward's face in my mind's eye, and I was consumed with hate, anger, rage, and murderous thoughts. It was very real.

I continued to pray to God, asking Him to make the forgiveness real. After a few more minutes, a loud roaring and sobbing escaped from deep within me! The intensity was frightening. But I wanted freedom. I gave in to what I felt God was doing. Besides, this wasn't something I had turned on, and I didn't have the power to turn it off. A prayer team person came by, and I just pointed at the box of tissues, as I was a mess, tears were streaming from my eyes, and my nose was dripping. She gave me the tissues and walked away. I cleaned up and closed my eyes, and I was crying out from the depths of my being, asking my God to help me.

I heard Mike praying over me again, "Take these things that bind Your daughter out by the roots, Lord, and set her free. Set her free in Your precious name!"

I don't know exactly how long I lay there crying, but it was quite some time. At some point, the underlying tone of anger changed, and I was weeping from all the broken places in me. My pleas had been ignored by so many adults who could've helped put a stop to things if only they had not turned a blind eye, or had believed me.

"You have made me willing, Lord, to forgive my father," I prayed as the crying calmed down. "You can touch and change my heart. Change my heart. Make it real, Oh, my Lord! I can't make it real! I agree with Mike's prayer, Lord, out by the roots! No more anger. No more rage and hate. No more murder. Freedom in Your mighty name, oh God!"

I felt like I had just had my own private counseling session with God, that He had given me all of His attention, and that He had touched me in a deep and powerful way! In my mind's eye, I saw Him take a surgical knife and lance my heart. Out of my heart oozed the pus of anger and hate and rage and murder and unforgiveness.

I had come to God with layers of all this junk and filth and sin, and I had acknowledged my anger toward Him. The Lord pursued me despite my anger towards Him, and He brought His healing, light, and peace to the hidden place within me. I was lying on the floor laughing as forgiveness rose up inside me. He was the only One who could make it real for me, and He had! Because of God's goodness and intervention in my life, abuse had no power over me anymore! I was no longer filled with inner turmoil and pain. I was overcome with a joy unspeakable. I would never, ever be the same! Freedom was mine! It was real! Holy and mighty God! What a gift He had given me. His Son had borne all that suffering on the cross that I might be free from all those things that had bound me for so long. I no longer ask, "Why me, Lord?" Now I ask, "What now, Lord?"

I look back to that night and am amazed at all the details that were taken care of so I could fully give my attention to what was happening in the moment. Bob was with the girls, so I was not worried about them or how long I was taking. The prayer team and leadership sensed God was doing something and let Him do His work without trying to help Him. I was so grateful to these people for their sensitivity. It was miraculous to me.

The Lord has healed me so that I may live fully in a world of words, expression, communication, and intimacy. After being silenced for the first fifteen years of my life, He led me to write as a means to share my story for the benefit of others who have known pain in a deep and crippling way, hoping to help them find their voices and freedom through knowing Christ. He spoke life and healing to all the broken places in my life and put me back together so I could be the person He had created me to be. He can do that for you too. Take the first step and fix your gaze upon Him and cry out to Him for help. I know He is faithful and good and kind and merciful. He will hear your prayers. He will give you freedom instead of bondage, joy instead of sorrow, laughter instead of anger, love instead of hate, and peace instead of torment. He will heal all your broken places and make you whole. He will help you change the end of your story.

I have been changed from the inside out, one memory at a time. Thanks be to God!

"The Spirit of the Lord is upon me; because

the Lord hath anointed me to preach good tidings to the meek;

He hath sent me to bind up the brokenhearted,

to proclaim liberty to the captives,

and the opening of the prison to them that are bound."

Isaiah 61:1

Epilogue

On November 22, 2019, I celebrated forty-two years of walking with the Lord. I continue to seek to be like Him and to honor Him with the choices I make on a day to day basis.

On March 22, 2020, I celebrated my 40th wedding anniversary to my best friend and covenant partner, Bob Newell. He's been by my side during this whole roller coaster ride.

I was told I would never have children. I'm so glad they were wrong. Bob and I have three wonderful daughters. I had the privilege of homeschooling them and teaching them to read. Seeing the world of words open up to them was one of my greatest joys! I left the workforce for twenty-three years so I could be home with them and assume the responsibility for their education. They are all unique and original, each pursuing her own dreams. I have a grandson and five granddaughters, and I treasure my time with them.

Over the course of my married life, I had met with several unique counselors during challenging seasons of my life. Each of them helped me embrace new levels of healing, spiritually, and emotionally. A couple of them were considered professional counselors, and a couple of them were people gifted more pastorally, able to listen and pray and encourage and push when needed. Each of them had assisted me in overcoming my abusive past.

I have had a life that none of my foster home counselors or my caseworker could ever have imagined for that broken girl who showed up at their front door many years ago.

Is everything in my life perfect? No. Do I still struggle with the residual effects of all the abuse I endured? I work in a chiropractor's office now, and one of my duties includes putting electrodes for electronic muscle therapy on our patients on their upper backs, mid-back, or lower back. To put the electrodes on the lower back, one has to set the electrodes down the back of the patient's pants. This very often exposes the top of the patient's butt. Just the other day, I thought I needed to put electrodes on the lower back of a male patient and had what seemed like a mini panic attack. It ended up with this patient that the electrodes only had to go on his upper back. But I went home crying with the residual apprehension I had felt with just thinking I might have to do that. My husband told me to talk to the chiropractor and explain. I talked with the doctor and my coworker the next day with tears streaming down my face and told them I couldn't handle anything that involves any private part of a man who isn't my husband. I was graciously told that I would not be asked to do that for our male patients. I felt an incredible sense of relief.

I am a work in process, and I am still learning to overcome and speak up for myself and to set boundaries in my life that help me feel safe.

I am so grateful for the life I've had, and I look forward to the days ahead!